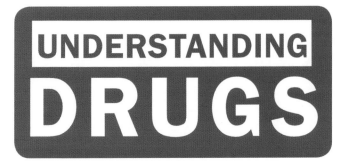

UNDERSTANDING DRUGS

Barbiturates and Other Depressants

TITLES IN THE *UNDERSTANDING DRUGS* SERIES

Barbiturates and Other Depressants

CHRISTINE ADAMEC

CONSULTING EDITOR:
DAVID J. TRIGGLE, Ph.D.
University Professor
School of Pharmacy and Pharmaceutical Sciences
State University of New York at Buffalo

CHELSEA HOUSE
PUBLISHERS
An imprint of Infobase Publishing

BARBITURATES AND OTHER DEPRESSANTS
Copyright © 2012 by Infobase Publishing

All rights reserved. No part of this book may be reproduced or utilized in any form
or by any means, electronic or mechanical, including photocopying, recording, or by
any information storage or retrieval systems, without permission in writing from the
publisher. For information, contact:

Chelsea House
An imprint of Infobase Publishing
132 West 31st Street
New York NY 10001

Library of Congress Cataloging-in-Publication Data

Adamec, Christine A., 1949–
   Barbiturates and other depressants / Christine Adamec ; consulting editor, David J.
Triggle. — 1st ed.
     p. cm. — (Understanding drugs)
   Includes bibliographical references and index.
   ISBN-13: 978-1-60413-534-3 (hardcover : alk. paper)
   ISBN-10: 1-60413-534-4 (hardcover : alk. paper)   1. Barbiturates.   I. Triggle, D. J.
II. Title.
   RM325.A33 2011
   615.7'821—dc23

                            2011027255

Chelsea House books are available at special discounts when purchased in bulk
quantities for businesses, associations, institutions, or sales promotions. Please call our
Special Sales Department in New York at (212) 967–8800 or (800) 322–8755.

You can find Chelsea House on the World Wide Web at
http://www.chelseahouse.com

Text design by Kerry Casey
Cover design by Alicia Post
Composition by Newgen North America
Cover printed by Yurchak Printing, Landisville, Pa.
Book printed and bound by Yurchak Printing, Landisville, Pa.

Printed in the United States of America

This book is printed on acid-free paper.
All links and Web addresses were checked and verified to be correct at the time of
publication. Because of the dynamic nature of the Web, some addresses and links may
have changed since publication and may no longer be valid.

Contents

foreword

THE USE AND ABUSE OF DRUGS

For thousands of years, humans have used a variety of sources with which to cure their ills, cast out devils, promote their well-being, relieve their misery, and control their fertility. Until the beginning of the twentieth century, the agents used were all of natural origin, including many derived from plants as well as elements such as antimony, sulfur, mercury, and arsenic. The sixteenth-century alchemist and physician Paracelsus used mercury and arsenic in his treatment of syphilis, worms, and other diseases that were common at that time; his cure rates, however, remain unknown. Many drugs used today have their origins in natural products. Antimony derivatives, for example, are used in the treatment of the nasty tropical disease leishmaniasis. These plant-derived products represent molecules that have been "forged in the crucible of evolution" and continue to supply the scientist with molecular scaffolds for new drug development.

Our story of modern drug discovery may be considered to start with the German physician and scientist Paul Ehrlich, often called the father of chemotherapy. Born in 1854, Ehrlich became interested in the ways in which synthetic dyes, then becoming a major product of the German fine chemical industry, could selectively stain certain tissues and components of cells. He reasoned that such dyes might form the basis for drugs that could interact selectively with diseased or foreign cells and organisms. One of Ehrlich's early successes was development of the arsenical "606"—patented under the name *Salvarsan*—as a treatment for syphilis. Ehrlich's goal was to create a "magic bullet," a drug that would target only the diseased cell or the invading disease-causing organism and have no effect on healthy cells and tissues. In this he was not successful, but his great research did lay the groundwork for the successes of the twentieth century, including the discovery of the sulfonamides and the antibiotic penicillin. The latter agent saved countless lives during World War II. Ehrlich, like many scientists, was an optimist. On the eve of World War I, he wrote, "Now that the liability to, and danger of, disease are to a large extent circumscribed—the efforts of chemotherapeutics are directed as far as possible to fill up the gaps left in this ring." As we shall see in the pages of this volume, it is neither the first nor the last time that science has proclaimed its victory over nature, only to have to see this optimism dashed in the light of some freshly emerging infection.

From these advances, however, has come the vast array of drugs that are available to the modern physician. We are increasingly close to Ehrlich's magic bullet: Drugs can now target very specific molecular defects in a number of cancers, and doctors today have the ability to investigate the human genome to more effectively match the drug and the patient. In the next one to two decades, it is almost certain that the cost of "reading" an individual genome will be sufficiently cheap that, at least in the developed world, such personalized medicines will become the norm. The development of such drugs, however, is extremely costly and raises significant social issues, including equity in the delivery of medical treatment.

The twenty-first century will continue to produce major advances in medicines and medicine delivery. Nature is, however, a resilient foe. Diseases and organisms develop resistance to existing drugs, and new drugs must constantly be developed. (This is particularly true for anti-infective and anticancer agents.) Additionally, new and more lethal forms of existing infectious diseases can develop rapidly. With the ease of global travel, these can spread from Timbuktu to Toledo in less than 24 hours and become pandemics. Hence the current concerns with avian flu. Also, diseases that have previously been dormant or geographically circumscribed may suddenly break out worldwide. (Imagine, for example, a worldwide pandemic of Ebola disease, with public health agencies totally overwhelmed.) Finally, there are serious concerns regarding the possibility of man-made epidemics occurring through the deliberate or accidental spread of disease agents—including manufactured agents, such as smallpox with enhanced lethality. It is therefore imperative that the search for new medicines continue.

All of us at some time in our life will take a medicine, even if it is only aspirin for a headache or to reduce cosmetic defects. For some individuals, drug use will be constant throughout life. As we age, we will likely be exposed to a variety of medications—from childhood vaccines to drugs to relieve pain caused by a terminal disease. It is not easy to get accurate and understandable information about the drugs that we consume to treat diseases and disorders. There are, of course, highly specialized volumes aimed at medical or scientific professionals. These, however, demand a sophisticated knowledge base and experience to be comprehended. Advertising on television is widely available but provides only fleeting information, usually about only a single drug and designed to market rather than inform. The intent of this series of books, **Understanding Drugs**, is to provide the lay reader with intelligent, readable, and accurate descriptions of drugs, why and how they are used, their limitations, their side effects and their future. The series will discuss both *"treatment drugs"*—typically, but not exclusively, prescription drugs, that have well-established criteria of both efficacy and safety—and *"drugs of abuse"* that have pronounced pharmacological and physiological effects but that are considered, for a variety of reasons, not to be considered for therapeutic purposes. It is our hope that these books will provide readers with sufficient information to satisfy their immediate needs and to serve as an adequate base for further investigation and for asking intelligent questions of health care providers.

—David J. Triggle, Ph.D.
University Professor
School of Pharmacy and Pharmaceutical Sciences
State University of New York at Buffalo

1
Overview

Gordon Weekley was a happily married father of four and a minister with adoring parishioners. Weekley had a bright future ahead of him in the church until one day in 1958 when he complained to his doctor about feeling jittery. The doctor prescribed both barbiturates and amphetamines—amphetamines to give him some "pep" and barbiturates to take the edge off the amphetamines so he could sleep. And thus began Reverend Weekley's 18-year descent into losing everything that he valued—his wife and children, his job, and nearly his life as well.

At first he liked the way the drugs made him feel—then later, Weekley needed them to feel normal. Dexamyl was one of his favorite drugs because it combined amobarbital, a barbiturate, with dextroamphetamine, a stimulant. Soon his regular dose wasn't enough, so Weekley began traveling to nearby cities to find doctors who would give him the extra prescriptions that he needed to feed his addiction. He perfected his cover story, which was that he was at a conference and had forgotten his shaving kit with his medications. He looked like a normal person and the doctors he consulted with gave him the prescriptions that he wanted, which he then filled at pharmacies away from home. According to his biographer, "Doctors weren't his only prey; he went after pharmacists, too. When a prescription would expire at a particular pharmacy, Gordon would go there anyway and act surprised when the person behind the counter told him he had no more refills. Somehow, some way, he would talk the pharmacist into one more."[1] It was only when Weekley admitted to himself that he could not handle these drugs anymore that

9

his healing process began, with the help of others who had faced the same drug problems.

A central nervous system **depressant** is a drug that slows down the brain by boosting the level of **gamma-aminobutyric acid (GABA).** GABA also appears naturally throughout the cells of the body as a fatty acid, and it is an inhibitory neurotransmitter.[2] As a result, the drug has a sedating effect rather than that excitatory effect that is seen with central nervous system stimulants, such as amphetamines. There are two main GABA receptors, including GABA-A and GABA-B. Most barbiturates and **benzodiazepines** affect GABA-A, while other depressants, such as gamma hydroxybutyric acid (GHB), affect GABA-B.

Barbiturates and benzodiazepines are two major categories of central nervous system (CNS) depressant drugs under the control of the Drug Enforcement Administration (DEA) because of their risk for abuse and addiction. These drugs are sedating and sleep-inducing ("hypnotic") prescription drugs. Barbiturates were developed in the 19th century with the creation of malonylurea by German chemist Adolf von Baeyer in 1864. The first **barbiturate** marketed in the United States was diethyl-barbituric acid (Veronal), introduced in 1904.[3] Benzodiazepine drugs were created in the mid-20th century by chemists for Hoffman LaRoche, a pharmaceutical company that had successes with the central nervous system depressant drugs Librium and Valium.

When barbiturates are used legitimately, they may be used to treat epilepsy, insomnia, anxiety, or severe chronic headaches. When barbiturates are abused, these drugs are often used to counteract the excitatory actions of stimulants that the abuser has taken illicitly, such as cocaine or methamphetamine.

When benzodiazepines are used legitimately, they are used to treat anxiety disorders. However, some people abuse benzodiazepines, for example, to experience euphoria. Benzodiazepines may be abused to potentiate (increase) the effects of alcohol, heroin, or other depressant drugs. They may also be abused to avoid withdrawal symptoms that will occur if use stops, as in the case of individuals who are addicted to benzodiazepines.

BARBITURATES

Barbiturate use and abuse is in sharp decline compared to past years, and the Drug Enforcement Administration reports that less than 10 percent of all depressant drugs that are prescribed in the United States are barbiturates.[4] Data from the Substance Abuse and Mental Health Services Administration (SAMHSA) in their analysis of sales of barbiturates over the period of 1998 to 2009 corroborate that statistic. According to SAMHSA, the sales of the formerly popular barbiturate phenobarbital plummeted from 3.7 million prescriptions in 1998 to 2.6 million in 2009.[5] In addition, the sales of butalbital fell even more dramatically, from 624,214 prescriptions written in 1998 to only 233,979 prescriptions in 2009. The Substance Abuse and Mental Health Services Administration reports that most individuals who are prescribed butalbital are males and females ages 41–50 years old, based on sales data that is available from pharmacies. (This information does not include information on people who obtain their barbiturates illegally.) According to SAMHSA, women are more likely than men to be prescribed this drug.

Barbiturates are classified in part on how rapidly they act in the body, and thus they may be categorized as ultra short-acting, short-acting, intermediate-acting, and long-acting, depending on how fast the drug causes a

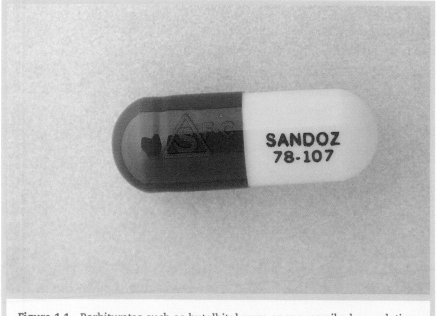

Figure 1.1   Barbiturates such as butalbital were once prescribed as sedatives and were popular drugs of abuse.   (© Custom Medical Stock Photo)

response in a person as well as how long the drug effect continues to work. When ultra short-acting drugs such as aprobarbital are used, they are administered intravenously as an anesthetic because of their very quick action on the patient. For example, an ultra short-acting barbiturate can put a person to sleep in about a minute from its intravenous administration, while it may take 15–40 minutes for a short or intermediate barbiturate to take effect. In contrast, a long-acting barbiturate like phenobarbital takes about 60 minutes to take its effect in the body, thus it is not the first choice for people who wish to abuse barbiturates.[6]

Most people who abuse barbiturates favor intermediate-acting drugs such as butalbital because they produce the rapid effects that they want. Nor do abusers want the almost instant sedation that leads to a state of unconsciousness.

Barbiturates Available Today

The primary barbiturates that are currently available for prescription are listed in Table 1.1, along with their brand names and their schedule classification received from the Drug Enforcement Administration (DEA). In addition, the table reflects whether these drugs are ultra short-acting, short-acting, intermediate, or long-acting barbiturates. In general, short-acting barbiturates such as pentobarbital (Nembutal) or secobarbital (Seconal) are Schedule II barbiturates, which is the highest schedule for legal drugs, while many other barbiturates are Schedule III drugs, such as butalbital and the key combinations of butalbital (Fiorinal, Fioricet). Some drugs containing barbiturates are suppositories and they are placed in an even lower drug category, or Schedule IV. Short- or intermediate-acting barbiturates are the most likely to be abused according to the Drug Enforcement Administration.

Current Uses of Barbiturates

Barbiturates are used by some people today as a treatment for epilepsy as well as a treatment for insomnia. In addition, some barbiturates are used to induce rapid sedation for preoperative sedation.

Some neurologists and other physicians prescribe barbiturates to treat chronic severe tension-type or migraine headaches, although other physicians have expressed serious concern about the addictive nature of these drugs. They also note that barbiturates may cause so-called rebound headaches, or headaches that are actually triggered by the chronic use of the medicine that

Table 1.1 Barbiturate Drugs and Abuse Schedule				
Generic Name	Brand Name	Ultra Short-Acting (U), Short/ Intermediate-Acting (SI) or Long-Acting (L)	Current DEA Schedule	Year First Approved by FDA
brevital	Methohexital	U	IV	1960
butabarbital	Butisol	SI	III	1939
phenobarbital suppository	Donnatol suppository	SI	IV	
pentobarbital	Nembutal	SI	II	1930
phenobarbital	Luminal (now generic only)	L	IV	1904
secobarbital	Seconal	SI	II	1929
thiopental	Pentothal	U	III	1930
Combination Drugs:				
acetaminophen, butalbital and caffeine	Esgic Plus, Fioricet	SI	III	1984
aspirin, butal-bital, and caffeine	Fortabs, Fiornal, Lanorinal, Phrenilin	SI	III	1976
Note: The Drug Enforcement Administration list of scheduled drugs include five schedules from Schedule I to Schedule V. Schedule I drugs are all illegal, while Schedule II–V drugs are legal but carry a risk of addiction. Legal drugs are classified in order of their risk for dependence, with Schedule II drugs having the most risk for addiction, followed by Schedule III and then Schedules IV and V.				
Source: Food and Drug Administration and Drug Enforcement Administration, "Controlled Substances by CSA Schedule," December 8, 2009.				

is taken to treat headaches.[7] This type of headache even has a specific classification, which is "medication-induced headaches." Such a situation may occur with the use of combination drugs such as Fiorinal, which combines butalbital (a barbiturate) with aspirin and caffeine. Medication-induced headaches may also occur with the chronic use of Fioricet, another drug that is a combination of butalbital, acetaminophen, and caffeine.

Side Effects and Adverse Effects

Even when they are used exactly as directed by a physician, barbiturates can cause sleepiness and dizziness in the user. At high dosages, these drugs can also cause breathing disorders, low blood pressure, a low sex drive, and a general lack of motivation. Elderly people who take barbiturates have an increased risk for falls. Barbiturates may also cause both positive and negative psychological effects. Positive effects include the relief from anxiety and sometimes a slight euphoria when the drug is used as directed. A negative effect from barbiturates may be memory problems. In addition, barbiturates may sometimes cause thoughts of suicide as well as feelings of paranoia.[8]

If barbiturates are abused or an individual becomes dependent on them, these drugs can be very dangerous and even fatal. According to the National Institutes of Health, when people accidentally overdose on barbiturates, whether they take excessive amounts of barbiturates alone or they take barbiturates in combination with other depressants, the death rate is about 10 percent. It is even higher if the individual does not receive prompt emergency medical treatment.[9]

If high levels of barbiturates are taken, this may lead to a condition that is known as acute barbiturate intoxication, a very dangerous state. Some symptoms of this condition may include staggering, slurred speech, uncoordinated movements, shallow breathing, and overall trouble with thinking. The person may also have a low body temperature (hypothermia) and low blood pressure (hypotension).[10] If the condition worsens, the kidneys may stop working and the person may need to receive kidney dialysis. Immediate medical attention is urgently needed in the case of **barbiturate intoxication.**

BENZODIAZEPINES

Some people refer to benzodiazepines as tranquilizers while others call them antianxiety medications or anxiolytics. Benzodiazepines enable many people to lead normal lives because the medication keeps their irrational fears or severe general anxiety in check and/or allows them to gain the sleep that they need. However, benzodiazepines can also become drugs of abuse. In the

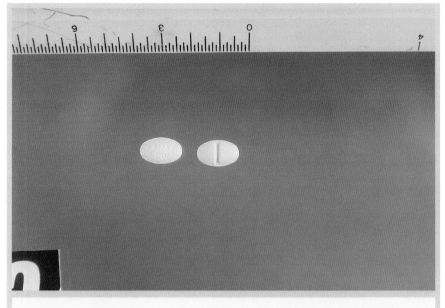

Figure 1.2 Alprazolam (Xanax) is a fast-acting benzodiazepine used to treat anxiety disorders; it also has a high potential for abuse. *(Drug Enforcement Administration)*

21st century, benzodiazepines have largely replaced barbiturates among those individuals who abuse central nervous system depressants other than alcohol.

Extent of Nonmedical Use of Benzodiazepines

According to the Substance Abuse and Mental Health Services Administration, in 2009, 9.2 million people ages 12 years and older used illicit drugs other than marijuana. Of these individuals, the majority, or 7 million, used psychotherapeutic drugs nonmedically. For example, 2 million people misused tranquilizers such as benzodiazepines, and 370,000 misused sedatives such as barbiturates.[11]

More than half of these nonmedical drug users said that they had obtained the drug from a friend or relative at no cost to themselves. They also noted that most of these friends or relatives originally had obtained the prescription for the drugs from a physician. This is referred to as **drug diversion,** which is the term for when a legitimately prescribed drug is given to another person

Table 1.2 Key Benzodiazepine Drugs and Schedules					
Generic Name	Brand Name	Short-Acting or Long-Acting	Drug Schedule	Year Approved by FDA
alprazolam	Xanax	L	IV	1981
chlordiazepoxide hydrochloride	Librium	L	IV	1960
clonazepam	Klonopin	L	IV	1975
clorazepate	Tranxene	L	IV	1972
diazepam	Valium	L	IV	1963
estrazolam	ProSom	S	IV	1990
flurazepam	Dalmone	S	IV	1970
halazepam	Paxipam	L	IV	1981
lorazepam	Ativan	L	IV	1977
midazolam	Versed (discontinued); generic available	S	IV	1985
nitrazepam	Mogadon		IV	
oxazepam	Serax	L	IV	1965
quazepam	Doral	L	IV	1985
temazepam	Restoril	S	IV	1981
triazolam	Triazolam (generic)	S	IV	1994
Combination Drugs:				
amitriptyline/ chlordiazepoxide	Limbitrol	L	IV	1977
amitriptyline/ chlordiazepoxide	Limbitrol DS	L	IV	1977

for abuse or misuse. The researchers also found that among new misusers of drugs ages 12–49 years in 2009, the average age of those who abused tranquilizers was 22.4 years and it was 19.7 years for those who abused sedatives. Finally, in 2009 among those ages 12 years and older, 481,000 individuals abused or were dependent on (addicted to) tranquilizers, while 147,000 abused or were dependent on sedatives.[12]

According to author Adam J. Gordon, M.D., in his book on physical illnesses and drugs of abuse, benzodiazepines that are used recreationally are rarely taken alone and instead, individuals who abuse benzodiazepines recreationally often take them with alcohol or other drugs, either to enhance their sedative effects or to counteract the effects of stimulants.[13]

Side Effects and Adverse Effects

Most benzodiazepines cause sleepiness and may also cause an overall "hungover" effect, as if the person had been out drinking heavily all night, even when no alcohol abuse had occurred. For example, they can cause sedation, impaired memory, a slowed motor response, and difficulty paying attention, as well as ataxia-like symptoms of difficulty with balance, coordination, and speech.[14] Benzodiazepines can also slow down the respiration rate, and if the individual is elderly, he or she has a greater risk for experiencing falls with this type of drug.

Abuse and addiction may occur if the person finds that, for example, one pill doesn't work as well as it did in the past, so the person decides (without consulting the doctor) to take two pills. Escalating the dosage will only worsen the **tolerance** problem and increase the risk for addiction.

Sales of Benzodiazepines Are High

Sales of benzodiazepine drugs have increased markedly since 1998, as illustrated in Table 1.3. For example, there was a 145 percent increase in the number of prescriptions for clonazepam (Klonopin) from 1998 to 2009, and an 85 percent increase in the number of alprazolam (Xanax) prescriptions. In considering the top 100 drugs of any type that were sold in the United States in 2009, five benzodiazepines made this list, including alprazolam (Xanax) at number 9 and clonazepam at number 31. Lorazepam (Ativan) was number 33, diazepam (Valium) was number 56, and temazepam (Restoril) was number 91.

Alprazolam appears to be a greater problem to consumers than other benzodiazepines because of its addictive potential and growing nonmedical use. Some doctors have noted that aggressive behavior and an increased risk of traffic accidents are linked to alprazolam use and they have also noted that withdrawal from alprazolam can be particularly difficult to undergo.[15]

ANXIETY DISORDERS: WHAT ARE THEY?

Because benzodiazepines may be used to treat **anxiety disorders** (as barbiturates were sometimes used in the past), it is a good idea to understand some basics about these disorders. Generalized anxiety disorder is an intense fear or dread that has no known source to the person experiencing it. Other anxiety disorders include panic disorder, obsessive-compulsive disorder, posttraumatic stress disorder (PTSD), and social phobia (also known as social anxiety disorder). Many of these disorders respond well to treatment with anxiolytic medications, although other medications such as antidepressants may also be used for treatment. Of course all forms of anxiety disorders are also treated with various types of psychotherapy.

Generalized Anxiety Disorder (GAD)

Generalized anxiety disorder (GAD) is a condition of constant worry and stress, even when there is nothing that is abnormally distressing that is occurring in the person's life. The individual with GAD constantly anticipates disaster and

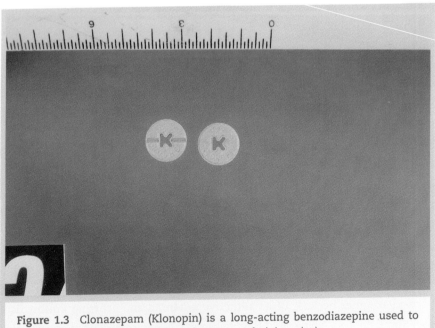

Figure 1.3 Clonazepam (Klonopin) is a long-acting benzodiazepine used to treat anxiety disorders. *(Drug Enforcement Administration)*

often has trouble falling asleep or staying asleep. Some physical symptoms that may accompany GAD include sweating, trembling, trouble with swallowing, headaches, muscle tension, and fatigue. Clonazepam (Klonopin) and alprazolam (Xanax) are benzodiazepines that are often used to treat GAD.[16]

Panic Disorder

Panic disorder is a very frightening anxiety disorder because it may feel like a heart attack to the individual, as it often includes such signs as a pounding heart, dizziness, faintness, perspiration, and a feeling of terror. Most panic attacks peak after about 10 minutes and then they subside, although attacks may last for a longer period. Alprazolam (Xanax) or extended release alprazolam (Xanax XR) are benzodiazepines that are often used to treat individuals with panic disorder, as is the benzodiazepine lorazepam (Ativan).[17] These two drugs are approved by the FDA to treat panic disorder. However, sometimes other high-potency benzodiazepines, such as triazolam (Halcion), are used off-label to treat individuals with panic disorder.[18]

Obsessive-Compulsive Disorder (OCD)

Obsessive-compulsive disorder (OCD) is an anxiety disorder that is marked by persistent thoughts as well as compulsive rituals that the person feels compelled to perform, even when they know that these thoughts and rituals are irrational. The thoughts and rituals are linked; for example, if the person is obsessively fearful of germs, then they may constantly and repeatedly wash their hands, sometimes until they are rubbed red and raw. OCD is often treated with antidepressants such as clomipramine (Anafranil), but its treatment may also be supplemented with benzodiazepines such as clonazepam (Klonopin), as well as with antipsychotics and other medications.[19] However, Jean-Marc Cloos, M.D., a psychiatrist specializing in addiction, notes that benzodiazepines should be used only in treatment-resistant cases of OCD.[20]

Post-Traumatic Stress Disorder (PTSD)

PTSD is an anxiety disorder that sometimes occurs after an extremely traumatic event, such as a combat experience, a sexual assault, extreme weather conditions such as a tsunami, a severe car accident, and other traumas to an individual. Individuals with PTSD may avoid places that may trigger traumatic memories of the event. Symptoms may include recurring nightmares

Table 1.3 Benzodiazepines Prescriptions, 1998–2009					
Drug	1998 Prescriptions Written	2009 Prescriptions Written	Percent Increase	2009 Ratio of Females to Males	Most Commonly Prescribed to
alprazolam	24.8 million	45.7 million	85%	2.1	Men and women ages 51–60 years
clonazepam	9.5 million	23.3 million	145%	1.8	Men and women ages 41–50 years
diazepam	11.9 million	14.4 million	21%	1.5	Men and women ages 51–60 years
lorazepam	17.2 million	22.6 million	32%	2.3	Females ages 71 and older, males 51–60 years
temazepam	6.2 million	9.1 million	46%	1.7	Men and women ages 71 years and older

Source: Sean J. Belouin, Pharm.D., and Janine Denis Cook, Ph.D., Clinical Chemist, Substance Abuse and Mental Health Services Administration, Twelve Year Prescribing Trends for Fifteen Different Opioid, Benzodiazepine, Amphetamine, and Barbiturate Prescription Drugs Correlated with Reports of Prescription Medication Abuse and Diversion (Presentation in 2010), http://www.benzos.une.edu/documents/2010/oct11/04_belouin.pdf (accessed on December 17, 2010).

and flashbacks of the traumatic event. The disorder is treated with antidepressants and sometimes with antipsychotic drugs. Psychiatrists may hesitate to treat this disorder with benzodiazepines because they may be fearful of the risk for addiction.[21]

Social Phobia

Social phobia, which is also known as social anxiety disorder (SAD), is a condition of extreme anxiety, stress, and self-consciousness when around other people. People with social phobia are very worried that others are watching them and judging them and they fear they may do something that will cause embarrassment to themselves. Clonazepam (Klonopin) is often used to treat social phobia. Sometimes beta blocker medications are used to treat this anxiety disorder. Antidepressants may also be used to treat social phobia.

OTHER DEPRESSANTS

Several other central nervous system depressants are worthy of discussion, including gamma hydroxybutyrate (GHB), flunitrazepam (Rohypnol), chloral hydrate, methaqualone (Quaalude), and paraldehyde.

Gamma-hydroxybutyrate (GHB)

First synthesized in the 1920s as an anesthetic, GHB is an illegal drug in the United States today.[22] It was placed in Schedule I as an illegal drug in 2000 because it has a high potential for abuse and has no legitimate medical purpose.[23]

The drug was previously sold as a means to bulk up muscle mass. It was also sometimes used as a date rape drug and was a colorless, odorless, and tasteless liquid put in an unknowing victim's drink so that the person could be sexually assaulted while unconscious.[24] GHB also comes in powder form. An estimated 1.4 percent of 12th graders in the United States said they had abused GHB in the past year, according to the 2010 *Monitoring the Future* survey.[25]

GHB is known as Bedtime Scoop, Georgia Home Boy, Great Hormones, Vita-G, and many other names.[26] Once taken, the drug acts within about 15 minutes and continues to act for up to four hours.

GHB does have one valid medical use. In rare cases, the drug sodium oxybate, which is chemically exactly the same as GHB, is used to treat a disorder known as narcolepsy under the brand name Xyrem.[27] Narcolepsy is a neurological disorder in which the brain cannot regulate sleep-wake cycles and as a result, people with narcolepsy uncontrollably lapse into sleep for periods of seconds to minutes. However, the use of Xyrem is tightly controlled and the incidents of diversion have been extremely rare: 1 in 5,200 patients, or less than 1 percent.[28] When sodium oxybate is used, the drug is scheduled as a Schedule III drug. Illicit GHB is a Schedule I drug.[29]

Flunitrazepam (Rohypnol)

Flunitrazepam is a benzodiazepine that is used for sedation and usually comes in pill form, although if abused sometimes it is ground up and snorted. When used illegally, it can be used as a date rape drug and is known as a "roofie." Flunitrazepam is sometimes used by individuals who abuse methamphetamine or cocaine so that they can sleep. The drug may cause aggression in some individuals. Flunitrazepam is not a legal drug in the United States. An estimated 1.5 percent of 12th graders used flunitrazepam in 2009, based on data from the 2010 *Monitoring the Future* survey.[30]

Flunitrazepam is also known as the Forget Pill, Mexican Valium, Mind Erasers, the Poor Man's Quaalude, and other names. The effects of Rohypnol occur within about 30 minutes of taking (or being given) the drug. The drug

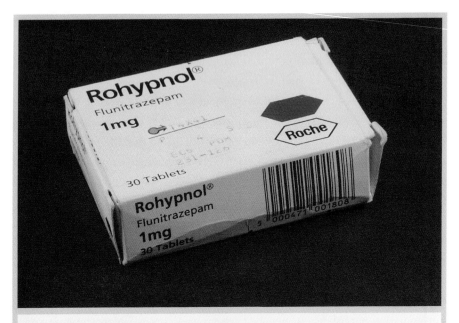

Figure 1.4 Flunitrazepam (brand name Rohypnol) is a benzodiazepine. It is most often taken as a pill, used as a sedative, but it is sometimes abused. It can be ground up and snorted by abusers. It is also the date rape drug known as "roofie." (© David Hoffman Photo Library/ Alamy)

can cause a lack of muscle control, dizziness, sleepiness, unconsciousness, confusion, amnesia, and even death.[31]

Chloral Hydrate

Chloral hydrate (brand name Aquacholoral) is a sedative that has several different uses. It is sometimes used to treat insomnia and it is also used to treat presurgery anxiety, especially in children. It is sometimes used after surgery to relieve pain. The drug comes in a capsule, liquid, or a rectal suppository. It can cause diarrhea, vomiting, and an upset stomach. Severe adverse reactions include confusion, trouble breathing, a slowed heartbeat, itching, and a rash. Individuals who have taken chloral hydrate should not drive a car or operate machinery.[32]

Methaqualone (Quaalude)

Methaqualone (brand name Quaalude) is a sedative hypnotic that was an extremely popular drug in the 1960s and was also a drug of abuse and addiction. First introduced in 1965 as a safe substitute for barbiturates, it was later discovered that methaqualone had a higher addiction potential than barbiturates, and that the withdrawal from methaqualone was similar to withdrawal from barbiturates. The drug was placed in Schedule I with other illegal drugs in 1991.[33] Methaqualone is still a drug of abuse in some countries, particularly South Africa and India, where the drug is smoked.

Paraldehyde

Paraldehyde is a central nervous system depressant that is used to cause sedation and also to treat acute and prolonged seizures that are resistant to other drugs. A 2009 study of rectally administered paraldehyde in 30 children over 53 episodes showed that the drug was both safe and effective in treating these seizures.[34] The chronic use or abuse of this drug can cause delusions, hallucinations, impaired memory, anxiety, tremors, and unsteady gait.[35]

2
Historical Background

Amy, 22, was very nervous although the reason for her problem had not been identified. It was 1950 and the doctor told her that a new drug would probably help calm her significantly. The doctor didn't tell Amy that the drug was a barbiturate, nor was he unusually remiss in this omission of information—doctors at that time often told patients what medicines to take without telling them what was actually in the drugs or what type of drugs they were. Their patients took them, usually without questioning the doctor any further.

Like others in her time, Amy took her medicine, asking no questions and assuming it would be fine. She did feel more relaxed after she started the drug, but after a few weeks, Amy found that if she missed taking her medicine for just a few days, she began to feel very anxious and distressed. She told the doctor about this, but he dismissed her complaint and told her she'd be fine, just keep taking the medicine. Amy developed a psychological dependence on the drug, and she assumed that she was somehow at fault for her need for the drug. She didn't know that it could be addictive.

The initial discovery of barbiturates is attributed to Adolf von Baeyer in 1864, when he synthesized malonylurea for the first time from the urea derived from the urine of animals and also from malonic acid that was derived from apples.[1] The drug was called a "barbiturate," and some say this was because von Baeyer was enamored of a woman named Barbara, while others say that he made his discovery on St. Barbara's Day. Still others say that the "barb" in

24

the word barbiturates primarily derived from the barbed appearance of the crystals that comprised the compound. No one really knows for sure which version of how these drugs received their name is the right one. Von Baeyer founded the company that later became the Bayer Chemical Company and he received the Nobel Prize in chemistry in 1905 for his work in advancing organic chemistry and the chemical industry.[2]

The first barbiturate was barbital (Veronal), introduced in Germany in 1903 and named after the Italian city of Verona. This drug was brought to the market because of the collaborative work of German chemists Josef Freiherr von Mering and Emil Fischer. (Fischer won the Nobel Prize in Chemistry in 1902.) Veronal was first manufactured by E. Merck in Germany and was available as cocoa-flavored tablets.[3]

Barbital was later followed by phenobarbital (Luminal) in 1911 and the subsequent development of many other barbiturates, such as Neonal, sold by Abbott Laboratories in 1922 (and no longer marketed today); Amytal (amobarbital) sold by Shonle and Moment in 1923; and then secobarbital (Seconal), first introduced by Shonle in 1929. In 1930, Abbott Laboratories introduced pentobarbital (Nembutal), followed by thiopental (Pentothal). Although sometimes known as truth serum, thiopental cannot compel people to tell the truth solely because they are drugged with this barbiturate. However, it can relax them sufficiently so that it might be easier in some cases to elicit truthful information from them. In general, when used today, thiopental is used as a preanesthetic.

THE FIRST BARBITURATES

The first barbiturates were introduced to sedate humans. In addition, some reports say that the Nazis used barbiturates to euthanize humans before World War II, prior to their use of nerve gas. For example, in one report, Nazi authorities approved euthanizing a severely handicapped institutionalized infant in 1939, using a fatal injection of the barbiturate Luminal. They subsequently drew up a list of mentally ill patients who should be euthanized, including those with schizophrenia, criminal insanity, epilepsy, Parkinson's disease, hereditary blindness, hereditary deafness, manic depression, and other ailments. Jewish patients were singled out for execution.[4]

During the mid-20th century, barbiturates were used primarily as antianxiety drugs as well as sedatives, anticonvulsants, and anesthetics. They were also combined in treatment with other drugs to treat diseases such as asthma or used by themselves to sedate individuals diagnosed with asthma.[5] In addition, barbiturates were used in the 1930s to treat individuals with high blood pressure, congestive heart failure, rheumatic fever, hyperthyroidism, and even peptic ulcers.[6]

Discoveries of Uses for Barbiturates

Because of their sedating effect, barbiturates were often used to treat individuals with insomnia, or, at higher dosages, as sedatives during surgery. Barbiturates have an anticonvulsant effect, which was an accidental finding credited to the German psychiatrist Alfred Hauptmann in 1912. At that time, Hauptmann was responsible for epileptic inpatients who had constant seizures, making it impossible for him or the patients to get any sleep. As a result, Hauptmann decided to give the then-new drug, phenobarbital, to his patients in an attempt to calm them down. He found that not only were the patients noticeably calmer but also the number of their seizures were significantly reduced, both at night and in the daytime.

Francisco López-Muñoz and colleagues in their article for *Neuropsychiatric Disease and Treatment* say that Hauptmann found that phenobarbital reduced the number of seizures as well as decreased their intensity. As a result, many patients were able to leave the institutions that they lived in and live normal lives.[7] However, because of the intrusion of World War I, the introduction of phenobarbital to the world, for seizures or any other treatments, was delayed until 1923.

Barbiturates were sometimes used for sedation before surgery in the 20th century, and sometimes also used as sedatives before surgical procedures. In his 1935 article on barbiturates. Dr. H. T. Roper-Hall wrote: "One of the great advantages of the barbiturates is their efficiency in the premedication of patients before operation; this can usually be carried out by giving a capsule orally an hour or two before operation, or in emergency, one of the sodium preparations, intravenously."[8]

Dr. Roper-Hall also noted that barbiturates could be given as antidotes to reactions to both cocaine and strychnine, stimulant drugs that were used to treat some patients in the early 20th century.[9] For example, strychnine or cocaine were sometimes used as stimulants in the treatment of individuals dying from pneumonia.

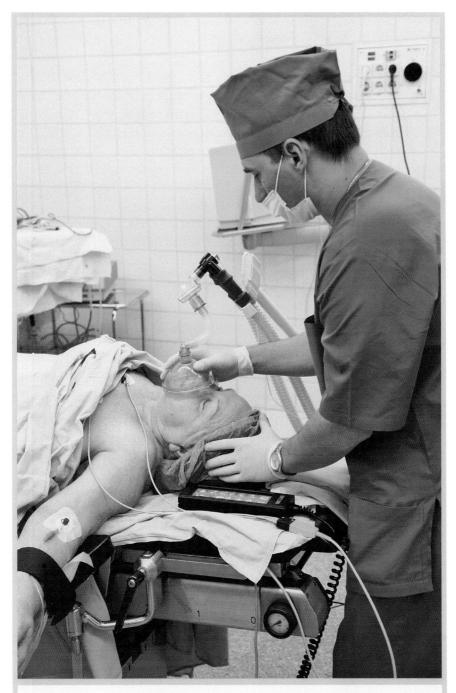

Figure 2.1 Certain barbiturates may be used for sedation before surgery. (© *shutterstock*)

THE DIVERSION OF BARBITURATES

Large quantities of barbiturates were produced in the 1940s and 1950s and some experts estimated that in 1951, half of all the barbiturates produced in the United States were diverted to illicit uses. Individuals in hotels, truck stops, and other sites sold barbiturates to willing buyers. One estimate is that there were probably about 50,000 people addicted to barbiturates in the early part of the 1950s.[13] By 1966, the FDA estimated that there were a half-million barbiturate abusers in the United States.[14]

According to historian Charles O. Jackson, in 1965, 9 billion barbiturate tablets were manufactured and it was likely that a significant part of this total production was diverted to illicit uses.[15]

In his 1952 article on the clinical use of barbiturates, Oliver F. Brust, M.D., stated that long-acting barbiturates could be used when a continued mild sedation was needed by a patient, as with those individuals who had such medical problems as hyperthyroidism, hypertension, nervous tension, and heart failure, as long as there was not any impairment of their kidney function.[10] Some doctors also recommended the use of intravenous barbiturates as a sedating treatment for patients diagnosed with terminal cancer.[11]

Barbiturates became very popular during and after World War II. Charles O. Jackson, in his article, "Before the Drug Culture," says that they were often given to wounded individuals in military hospitals. Barbiturates were also used as therapy for patients with combat fatigue, to help them more readily talk about their traumatic experiences in combat.[12]

The Use of Barbiturates as Therapy or Truth Drugs

In the mid-20th century, so-called truth serums, or sodium pentothal and amobarbital, were used by several different groups in their attempts to elicit the truth. Some Freudian psychiatrists used the drugs in an attempt to delve more deeply into the patient's unconscious mind in order to identify past traumatic events that might be causing current neuroses. It was believed by some experts at the time that by confronting these past traumas, the patient would experience what Freud called "abreaction," which was a sort of "Aha!" moment that Freud believed would cure a neurotic individual. This type of treatment, combining drugs with therapy, was sometimes referred to as "narcotherapy."[16]

In addition, psychiatrists believed that the drug was useful with severely mentally ill individuals. In 1946, psychiatrist Burgess E. Moore said in the *Yale Journal of Biology and Medicine:* "Under massive doses of chloral and the various barbiturates, which has been introduced by Emil Fischer in 1903, it was observed that psychotic patients seemed to be in better contact with the physician and would often reveal information pertinent to their emotional state without remembering it later. This provided material with which the physician could work in his psychotherapeutic attempts with the patient."[17]

Some experts believed that the barbiturate amobarbital was superior to pentothal for the treatment of patients. For example, Maria Naples and Thomas P. Hackett described the historical use of amobarbital in their 1978 article for *Psychosomatics.* These authors said that amobarbital was first used in 1930 to treat psychiatric disorders, primarily in the case of treatment of manic depressive (bipolar) patients who were extremely excited to the point of physical exhaustion. The drug helped them sleep while in a manic state or in an agitated depressive state.[18]

Then in 1932, psychiatrist Erich Lindemann reportedly gave patients a sufficient amount of amobarbital to sedate them but not cause unconsciousness. Lindemann found that patients who were unable to communicate with their doctors prior to the administration of the drug were subsequently able to share their thoughts with the doctor after it was given.

In World War II, amobarbital was given to soldiers suffering with acute war neurosis, which is a condition that is now referred to as post-traumatic stress disorder (PTSD). This condition can result from very extreme trauma, such as combat stress as well as other forms of extreme stress, such as rape and very severe states of physical or emotional deprivation.[19]

After the war, amobarbital was given to patients to help them accept their need for treatment and to reveal their underlying thoughts that were concealed from the therapist.[20] Some doctors used the drug to treat medical problems that were resistant to therapy, such as gastric ulcers. Such treatment was doomed to failure because it is now known that most gastric ulcers are caused by a bacterium, *Helicobacter pylori,* or by the chronic use of nonsteroidal anti-inflammatory drugs (NSAIDs). At that time, however, it was believed that it was stress alone that caused most ulcers.[21]

These drugs were also used by some law enforcement officials to elicit confessions to crimes, although many courts threw out any criminal confessions that were taken while an individual was under the influence of drugs.[22] However, some organizations and individuals believed that the so-called truth serum was an important and useful tool, and as a result, some courts requested psychiatrists at Bellevue Hospital, a psychiatric hospital in New York City, to inject accused murderers with amobarbital in order to determine if they were actually faking their mental illness. The involved patients had no say in whether they were injected with the drug.[23]

During World War II, the Central Intelligence Agency (CIA) and military organizations experimented with the use of sodium pentothal and sodium amobarbital, as part of Operation Bluebird in 1950, renamed Operation Artichoke in 1951, in attempts to use the drugs as truth serums. Earlier experiments were performed in 1948 on unsuspecting army soldiers in order to explore the effects of the drugs. In another study, according to Laura Calkins, subjects were ordered to memorize lies and then they were given barbiturates to see if they could still lie while under the influence of drugs. The result: they could lie and they did. Thus, although sedating barbiturates did relax patients significantly, in general it did not necessarily elicit truthful responses.[24]

BARBITURATES THROUGH THE 20TH CENTURY

From the standpoint of the consumption of drugs alone, barbiturate drugs such as phenobarbital, secobarbital, amobarbital, pentobarbital, and thiopental were popular drugs through the 1960s and 1970s. According to the American Medical Association's Committee on Alcoholism and Addiction, in their published statement in the *Journal of the American Medical Association* in 1965, approximately 1 million pounds of barbituric acid was produced in 1962 alone, which was said to be enough to provide 24 100-mg doses of barbiturates to every man, woman, and child living in the United States in that year.[25]

Barbiturates were also very popular in Europe; for example, according to Frank Wells in his 1976 article for the *Journal of Medical Ethics,* an estimated 11 million prescriptions were written for barbiturates in England alone in

1971, and 16,000 patients had been admitted to hospitals for an overdose of barbiturates. Of those patients, 2,000 died.[26]

Barbiturates were drugs that were available without a prescription in the United States until 1951, when the Durham-Humphrey Amendment required that these drugs be prescribed by physicians only.[27] However, the enforcement was reportedly very lax until after the passage of the Controlled Substances Act in 1970.

AN EARLY DISCUSSION OF INDUCED BARBITURATE ADDICTION

In 1940, Harris Isbell and his colleagues reported on their experimentation on five former morphine addicts and their subsequent responses to an induced addiction to barbiturates. Isbell and his staff administered high dosages of such barbiturates as pentobarbital, secobarbital, and amobarbital to their subjects, providing these drugs to their subjects for a range of from 92 to 144 days. When the barbiturates were withdrawn from the subjects, the researchers then noted that four of the five subjects experienced convulsions, and that four of the subjects also experienced psychotic features.[28] (Such experiments would not be considered ethical in the 21st century.)

These authors said of their findings, "One of the most striking features of chronic barbiturate intoxication in the experiment of Isbell was the great variation in the effect of the barbiturates in different individuals and in the same individual on different days. One man who took 1.8 to 2.0 grams of Seconal [secobarbital] daily exhibited only mild to moderate signs of intoxication while another individual who was receiving only 1.3 grains of Seconal daily can best be described as a staggering drunk. On certain days, a dose of barbiturate would produce little effect in a given individual and on other days the same dose would cause severe intoxication and even light coma."[29] This research showed that it was possible to become addicted to barbiturates, which later research confirmed.

ABUSE OF BARBITURATES

In the 1930s, barbiturates were popular as drugs of abuse. According to author Charles O. Jackson, the Food and Drug Administration (FDA) became alarmed by the number of traffic accidents that were associated with barbiturate abuse, as did some states, and consequently, 16 states markedly restricted the sales of barbiturates by the end of the 1930s.[30] At that time, the FDA had little power and instead the states primarily regulated drug use, in contrast to the situation today in which both the federal and state governments work against drug trafficking and illegal drug use.

Barbiturate production continued apace for years, from the production of 531,000 pounds of barbiturates in 1941 to the high of 900,000 pounds in 1947. Some of this was related to World War II, when barbiturates were used to sedate wounded soldiers, treat combat fatigue, and comfort the dying.[31] Pharmacists were sometimes part of the problem because they failed to check to see whether so-called refills that were requested by the patient had actually been ordered by the doctor. Author Charles O. Jackson cited the case of a woman in Kansas City who was found dead of barbiturate poisoning, as a result of a mail order drugstore from which she had received an estimated 7,000 barbiturate capsules by mail over the course of five years. The drugstore shipping the drugs had never checked to see whether the doctor had actually ordered these refills. (He had not.)[32] Such a situation is unlikely to occur today, although it is true that some people illegally order prescription drugs from the Internet in the 21st century.

It has been known for many years that barbiturates can be addicting, although there are indications that some doctors ignored the signs of addiction, while in other cases, addicted patients became very clever at doctor shopping—seeing multiple doctors in order to obtain prescriptions at multiple pharmacies. In his discussion of the addiction to barbiturates published in 1952, Oliver F. Bush wrote the following:[33]

> Habituation to the barbiturates is now widespread, and this type of addiction resembles that of alcoholism and narcotic addiction in many respects. Treatment may be very difficult if the patient has been taking large amounts of barbiturates for any length of time. Almost all barbiturate addicts use the short acting drugs; therefore, in order to avoid the creation of new addicts, it is recommended that only the long acting drugs be prescribed if treatment over a prolonged interval is indicated. If the short acting drugs are used it is recommended that they be prescribed in small quantities and the indications for their use frequently reviewed.

THE PROCESS OF ADDICTION TO BARBITURATES AND AMPHETAMINES

Historian Charles Jackson described the process by which many people became addicted to barbiturates along with amphetamines in the 1960s: "This was the housewife or business man who cannot sleep and so obtains a prescription for a barbiturate. Since the drug induced depression is still making itself felt the next morning, the patient has a hangover. The physician now turns to amphetamines—something to counter the barbiturate and to get the patient started on the new day. In a few weeks the patient may be completely dependent upon the artificial moods his doctor has provided."[34]

Congress became so concerned about barbiturate abuse nationwide that a hearing on barbiturate abuse, chaired by Senator Edward Kennedy, was held in 1973. According to this report, amobarbital, pentobarbital, and secobarbital were among the 10 most abused drugs in the United States at that time.[35]

One of the individuals who testified at this hearing, Dr. Donald R. Wesson, described a means by which some drug abusing individuals obtained their drugs, a strategy that is also known as "doctor shopping" in the 21st century:[36]

The one behavioral pattern which distinguishes members of the middle class or upper middle class, who use tranquilizers or even barbiturates advantageously to combat excessive anxiety or stress, is the tendency of some individuals to increase the dose on their own without the doctor's knowledge. As they increase their daily dosage, they frequently begin visiting other physicians. Many times several physicians end up prescribing for these patients, each without the knowledge of the others. I believe this is also very important because each of these physicians may believe in all sincerity that the patient they are prescribing for is not a barbiturate abuser. When he reviews his records, he says this particular patient is not using in excess of therapeutic dosages, which I am prescribing. Unfortunately, this

HEROIN ADDICTS WHO USED BARBITURATES

In a study on heroin addicts who also used barbiturates, published in 1968 in the *Canadian Medical Association Journal,* the researchers studied 30 addicts, including 16 men and 14 women. The addicts were asked why they used barbiturates, and 43 percent of the males and 35 percent of the females said a key reason was their inability to obtain heroin; thus barbiturates were a second choice of drug. Twenty-five percent of the males (and none of the females) said they used barbiturates to potentiate (increase) the effect of alcohol. In addition, the addicts also said that they used barbiturates about 20 minutes before they injected heroin to potentiate the effect of the injected heroin. This is a very risky practice, because if the heroin the individual uses is purer than the individual realizes, they risk coma or death with the combination of both the barbiturate and the heroin.[37]

patient is using four to six physicians in the same way, none of whom may realize the patient is abusing the drug.

Now, it has been our experience that pharmacists have been most often the ones to discover that, well, Mrs. Jones is getting prescriptions from Dr. A and Dr. B and Dr. C. If Mrs. Jones is smart, she will take her prescriptions to various drug stores, and this pattern may go on literally for months to 4 or 5 years before the patient develops a pattern of addiction which is so heavy that she cannot function in her usual capacity, at which time her addiction is discovered, perhaps by one of her treating physicians.

CHILDREN AND BARBITURATES

Barbiturates were used in past years for children who had anxiety. Barbiturates have also been used with children diagnosed with cyclic vomiting, a disorder of recurrent vomiting with no known cause. In fact, this treatment was used from the 1950s until the end of the 20th century.[38] In his 1997 article on barbiturates that were used to treat cyclic vomiting in children, published in the

Journal of Pediatric Gastroenterology & Nutrition, Dr. R. Gokhale reported on his study of 14 children with this disorder over the long-term period 1984 to 1995. He noted that the vomiting was extreme enough that the children were hospitalized for diagnosis and treatment; however, the diagnostic studies that they received ruled out any physical abnormalities in the children.

The children were prescribed phenobarbital daily and, according to Gokhale, 11 subjects recovered completely and three improved significantly. The conclusion was that barbiturate treatment was effective.[39]

A much more common use of barbiturates in children in the mid-20th century was to use the drug to treat the febrile seizure, a seizure which may occur with the sudden spiking of a fever in an ill child. Some doctors believed in the immediate hospitalization of such children while others recommended the initiation of phenobarbital for at least a six-month period. Still other doctors continued treatment with phenobarbital until the child was age five or six.[40] Today doctors no longer automatically assume that children experiencing one or more fever-induced seizures must have epilepsy, nor do doctors treat children who are not diagnosed with epilepsy with barbiturates.

DECREASING BARBITURATE CONSUMPTION IN LATE 20TH CENTURY

Barbiturate consumption declined markedly in the later 20th century to the 21st century; for example, according to the SAMHSA, the number of phenobarbital prescriptions plummeted by 28 percent from 1998 to 2009, or from about 3.7 million prescriptions in 1998 to 2.6 million in 2009. In addition, the percentage of butalbital prescriptions dropped by 63 percent within this same time period, or from about 624,000 in 1998 to 234,000 by 2009.[41]

The major reason for this decline apparently was the overwhelming popularity of a new type of drug that appeared on the horizon starting in the mid-20th century and one that many physicians believed was much safer and with no addictive potential: benzodiazepine drugs.

Some researchers, such as author Edward Shorter, reported the belief that the underlying kiss of death for most barbiturates occurred in 1972 when the Bureau of Narcotics and Dangerous Drugs (precursor to the Drug Enforcement Administration) moved barbiturates to Schedule II drugs from the lower level of Schedule III. As a result, most physicians allegedly became fearful of prescribing barbiturates, and thus, the heyday of these drugs was over.[42] Note that today most barbiturates are Schedule III drugs and barbiturates are no longer popular drugs of abuse.

BETWEEN BARBITURATES AND BENZODIAZEPINES: MEPROBAMATE

Some researchers believe that the introduction of meprobamate (Miltown, Equanil) was a sort of dress rehearsal for the subsequent development and marked success of benzodiazepine medications in the United States. Referred to as a tranquilizer, and prescribed for anxiety, meprobamate was a depressant drug that was first marketed in 1954, and it became rapidly popular among many people in the United States.[43] This drug was accidentally discovered by German researcher Frank Berger in Britain, when he was researching antibiotics and discovered its tranquilizing effects.[44]

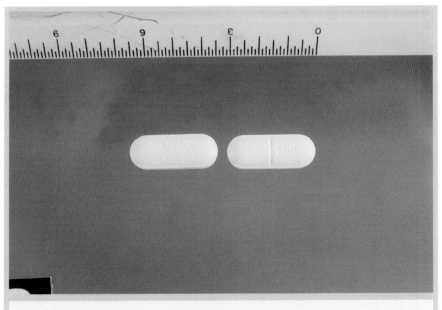

Figure 2.2 Meprobamate is a tranquilizing depressant drug that was first marketed in 1954 under the brand name Miltown. *(Drug Enforcement Administration)*

The demand for the drug was high, and some pharmacies had signs in the window "We have Miltown."[45] Comedian Milton Berle told a reporter for *Time* magazine in 1956 that he was thinking of changing his name to Miltown Berle, because the drug was so effective.[46] However, it eventually became clear that the drug had problematic side effects as well as an addictive potential, and consequently, other options were sought. Miltown was withdrawn from the market in 1965.[47] (Other forms of meprobamate are available today.) What came next was perceived as the next best thing: the benzodiazepine drugs.[48] As with many other prior drugs, it was initially believed that benzodiazepines were drugs with few side effects and no addictive potential. Sadly, this belief was disproven.

THE HISTORY OF BENZODIAZEPINES

The formula for the first benzodiazepine was developed by Leo Sternbach, a chemist for pharmaceutical company Hoffman-LaRoche who was relocated by the company to the United States from Switzerland in 1940 because he was a Jew who was ordered to leave the country. It turned out to be a very profitable decision for the company.

According to author Andrea Tone, Sternbach first worked on synthesizing vitamins, having great success. Then in the 1950s, he was told to work on creating a tranquilizer. Sternbach created at least 40 different benzoheptoxidazine derivatives, which were chemicals he had worked on as a student in the University of Krakow in the 1930s, but none of his derivatives were tranquilizing. Sternbach and a colleague decided to use methylamine to treat one of his derivatives, creating a white powder. He labeled it as Ro 5–0690, setting it aside and then forgetting about it. By 1956, the company told Sternbach to give up and start working on creating antibiotics.[49]

Then in 1957, while cleaning his laboratory, Sternbach found the compound again. He thought about throwing it out. At the urging of his colleagues, Sternbach sent the sample for testing to Dr. Lowell Randall, who was the chief of pharmacology for Hoffman-LaRoche.

Randall tested the compound and found it was highly tranquilizing on mice and cats. He also found it was more sedating and less dangerous than other sedating drugs on the market. The company named the drug "Librium" for the end of "equilibrium." Sternbach further researched and discovered that he had unknowingly created a new chemical that had no relation to his other derivatives. Sternbach had created the benzodiazepine. Clinical trials for Librium began in 1958.[50]

The drug chlordiazepoxide hydrochloride (Librium) was first approved by the Food and Drug Administration in 1960 and diazepam (Valium) subsequently received FDA approval in 1963. In 1960, other tranquilizers such as Miltown, Stelazine, Thorazine, Compazine, and Equanil held 70 percent of the tranquilizer market, but Librium quickly became very popular and in its first year of introduction, this drug took over 20 percent of the tranquilizer market. However, the drug had a bitter aftertaste, and its developer, chemist Leo Sternbach, worked on creating a stronger and better-tasting benzodiazepine, eventually developing both clonazepam (Klonopin) and flurazepam (Dalmane). Sternbach was also the developer of diazepam (Valium), which ultimately became a blockbuster success for his employer, pharmaceutical company Hoffman-LaRoche.[51] Sternbach died in 2005 at the age of 97 years. He spent his entire 33-year career at Hoffman-LaRoche.[52]

When Librium was first introduced, it was believed to be effective with many medical problems, including gastrointestinal pain, muscle spasms, alcoholic hallucinations, and anxiety. By March 1966, more than 15 million individuals had taken 6 billion capsules of Librium, and it was the second most prescribed drug among elderly individuals.[53]

Benzodiazepines became so popular worldwide in the 1960s that they were used for a myriad of problems, including anxiety, insomnia, hypertension, heart disease, and even bipolar disorder (then known as manic depression) and schizophrenia. In fact, if the doctor could not find a cause for the patient's symptoms, then there was a fairly good chance that a benzodiazepine would be considered. For example, in Germany at this time, the following maxim was allegedly adopted by some physicians: "Wenn man nicht weiss, wie, was, warum, dann gibt man immer Valium." Which means, "When you don't know how, what and why, it's time for Valium."[54]

Valium began to eclipse Librium in the 1970s and by 1972, 50 million prescriptions a year were written for Valium, in contrast to 4 million prescriptions in 1964. The patent for Valium expired in 1985 and the drug then appeared as a generic drug all around the globe under many different names.[55]

Concern about benzodiazepines began to be expressed in many forms of media. In 1978, in a stunning admission, the former First Lady Betty Ford publicly stated that she had a problem with alcohol and tranquilizers (Valium),

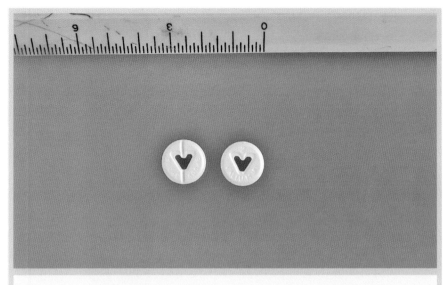

Figure 2.3 Valium, a benzodiazepine and tranquilizer, was first approved by the FDA in 1963. *(Drug Enforcement Administration)*

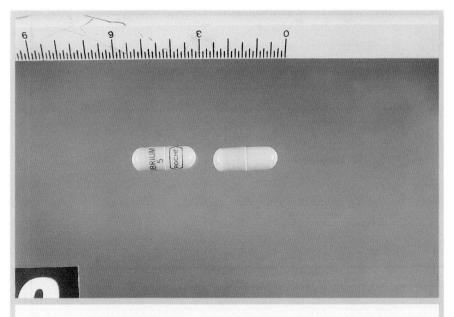

Figure 2.4 Librium (chlordiazepoxide hydrochloride), the first benzodiazepine, was discovered in 1957 by chemist Leo Sternbach while working for Hoffman-LaRoche. *(Drug Enforcement Administration)*

and urged others with this problem to get help.[56] Author Barbara Gordon wrote that her doctor urged her to take stronger tranquilizers in her book *I'm Dancing As Fast as I Can,* published in 1979. In 1979, Senator Edward Kennedy, who in earlier years had held hearings on the issue of barbiturate abuse, led a Senate investigation on whether the existing controls on tranquilizers (benzodiazepines) were sufficient.[57] Numerous magazine articles and television and radio shows expressed concern about the risks generated by benzodiazepines.

BENZODIAZEPINES TODAY

Although use and abuse of barbiturates has fallen off, doctors continue to prescribe benzodiazepines for anxiety, insomnia, and sometimes for other medical or psychiatric problems. In their analysis of physician prescriptions for benzodiazepines from July 2007 to June 2008, researchers Elisa Cascade and Amir H. Kalali found that 112.8 million prescriptions for benzodiazepines were filled. Of these prescriptions, most (55 percent) were written by a primary care physician, while 16 percent were prescribed by a psychiatrist and 29 percent were prescribed by other specialist physicians. When considering treatment for anxiety alone, primary care physicians were more likely to prescribe a benzodiazepine alone for this problem (42 percent) than were psychiatrists (22 percent).[58]

OTHER DEPRESSANTS

In addition to barbiturates and benzodiazepines, there are also other depressants that have been used legitimately at some time, as well as having been used as drugs of abuse and dependence. Some of the drugs have been available for more than a hundred years. For example, chloral hydrate was first used as a sedative in 1869.[59]

Gamma-hydroxybuytrate (GHB)

GHB is a drug that has been used by athletes in the past to build muscle mass. GHB is abused to induce euphoria and enhance sociability and sexuality. It was initially developed as an anesthetic but that use was abandoned. Abuse of the drug can lead to loss of consciousness, coma, and death. Other effects may be involuntary muscle jerking, a heightened tactile sense, visual and auditory hallucinations, extreme anxiety, confusion, sleeplessness, and fatigue.[60, 61]

Flunitrazepam (Rohypnol)

Flunitrazepam is a benzodiazepine that was introduced in 1975. Rumors and reports of misuse of the drug occurred and the drug was moved from Schedule IV to Schedule III in 1995. Flunitrazepam is swallowed or snorted. It has been used as a date rape drug because it is colorless and odorless and can render the victim unconscious and incapable of resisting an assault.

Chloral Hydrate

German chemist Justus von Liebig first synthesized chloral hydrate in 1832, but the drug was not introduced until 1869 by German pharmacologist Oskar Liebreich. It was used as a sedative and treatment for insomnia.[62] Still used

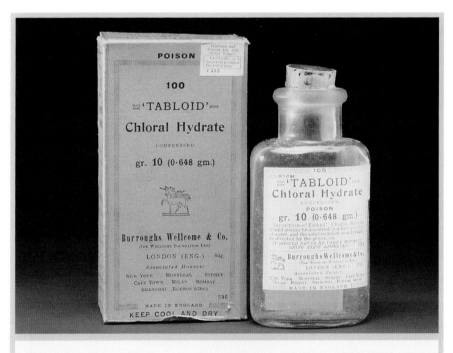

Figure 2.5 Chloral hydrate was first used as a sedative and insomnia drug in 1869. It is still used today as a preoperative sedative for children. (©SSPL/ Getty Images)

Figure 2.6 Paraldehyde was first used by doctors as a sedating drug in 1882. (© Vintagemedical.com)

today to sedate children, chloral hydrate is a sedative with a long track record. In the late 19th century, it was used as a substitute for morphine, since it did not require injection and could be given to patients in the home.[63] Chloral hydrate was first used with a pediatric population in 1894, and in 2003, was listed as the seventh most frequently chosen drugs for sedation in children. The drug may be administered orally or rectally and is well tolerated for short-term or one-time use. However, patients of all ages should be monitored for any respiratory or cardiac changes.[64] If the drug is used for a prolonged period, it can lead to tolerance and a need for higher doses to achieve the same result, and these results have been reported in both adults and children.

Methaqualone (Quaalude)

Methaqualone was a drug of abuse and dependence in the 1970s. Some young people used the drug with wine, increasing its depressant effect. The drug was swallowed or injected. In other countries in the world such as South Africa today, methaqualone is smoked. The drug was placed in Schedule I in 1984, making it illegal to possess this drug in the United States.

Paraldehyde

Paraldehyde was first used by clinicians in 1882 as a sedating drug.[65] In the past, paraldehyde was also used to treat alcoholism but it is no longer used for this purpose, in part because some alcoholics switched their addiction choice from alcohol to paraldehyde. In addition, better treatment drugs were developed for alcoholism.

3

How Barbiturates and Other Depressants Work

Amy, age 28, was an alcoholic who also depended on her daily dosage of diazepam (Valium). She knew that she shouldn't mix alcohol with her Valium but sometimes she felt so depressed and so angry with the world that she wanted to shut everything and everybody out. She had made some bad life choices; for example, the state had taken away Amy's baby for neglect. What happened was a neighbor called the police because the baby was screaming so long, and when the neighbor rang the doorbell and pounded on the door, Amy didn't answer. She didn't answer because she was in a deep sleep after drinking and taking several Valium pills, and couldn't hear the neighbor or her baby or anything else. In fact, she was so deeply asleep that the cops took her to the emergency room to make sure she was okay. When she recovered, Amy promised with all her heart it would never happen again. But then she got really upset because she broke up with her boyfriend and things just seemed so awful. So she had a few drinks and also swallowed a few extra Valiums, again ignoring her child's hysterical screams. This time when the neighbor called the police and the social worker talked to Amy, the caseworker seemed a lot less receptive to Amy's problem and told Amy that the child was being placed in a foster home for his safety.

Both barbiturates and benzodiazepines are central nervous system depressants, and both work by increasing the effect of gamma-aminobutyric acid (GABA), the primary neurotransmitter in the central nervous system that inhibits activity. GABA is a sort of slowing-down mechanism, and when there is not sufficient GABA, then an individual experiences emotional and/ or physical stress. Individuals with chronic anxiety disorders may suffer from low levels of GABA.[1] For example, researchers tested the GABA levels of individuals who were involved in traffic accidents and assessed them for the presence of the post-traumatic stress disorder (PTSD), an anxiety disorder, six weeks later. They found that the average GABA level in the PTSD group subjects was significantly lower compared to those who were exposed to trauma but did not develop PTSD. As a result, low post-traumatic GABA blood levels may be predictive for the development of acute PTSD.[2]

Some experts believe that some autoimmune diseases such as multiple sclerosis may be caused by a low level of GABA,[3] while others believe that the underlying key to autism may lie at least in part with a low level of GABA or of GABA receptors.[4] Future research will provide more information that may help with treatment of these disorders.

There are two primary GABA receptors, including GABA-A, the main receptor for barbiturates and benzodiazepines and many other drugs, and GABA-B, a receptor for the drug gamma hydroxybutyrate (GHB). The neurotransmitter GABA is present throughout the brain and affects the entire central nervous system. It is primarily produced in the cerebral cortex of the brain.[5] Throughout life, there is a constant chemical interaction between the brain and body that affects neurotransmitter production or sometimes that overrides the actions of neurotransmitters. For example, if the individual becomes excessively excited, GABA helps to calm the person down. Actions that a person takes can affect GABA levels. For example, if a person consumes stimulants such as caffeine or amphetamine, these substances work to override the inhibitory effect of naturally produced GABA.

GABA that is produced from within the person's brain can only be boosted by the effects of some drugs, such as barbiturates and benzodiazepines or GHB. Individuals that take supplements of GABA may feel better, and this may be largely because they think that they will feel better. This is known as the placebo effect, which means that in studies, even when some subjects receive the placebo, or sugar pill, rather than the tested drug, they report feeling better.

Barbiturates act directly on GABA and also block excitatory signals by preventing the action of alpha-amino-3-hydroxyl-5-methyl-4-isoxazole-propionate (AMPA) receptors. These actions together cause a depression/

sedation of the central nervous system.[6] Benzodiazepines are also drugs that sedate the central nervous system, but they act in a different chemical way from barbiturates. After the benzodiazepine is taken, the drug is modified within the body by the action of specific enzymes that are known as cytochrome P450 enzymes.

Some benzodiazepines are primarily metabolized by CYP3A4, a cytochrome P450 enzyme, while others are partially metabolized by this enzyme.[7] The metabolites from this action are then circulated throughout the central nervous system, where they act on neurotransmitter receptors that are sensitive to GABA.

Barbiturates act directly on GABA receptors in the central nervous system, while benzodiazepines act indirectly through their interaction with GABA.[8] However, the bottom line is barbiturates and benzodiazepines, as well as other depressants, boost the level of GABA and cause an inhibition of the central nervous system. For example, barbiturates enhance the action of GABA by binding to the GABA-A receptor, which is located near the chloride entrance of a neuron. Thus, they cause a channel to open up, allowing negatively charged chloride ions to flow over the membrane. This action boosts the sedating effects that natural GABA provides.[9] Benzodiazepines act on a different part of the GABA-A receptor than barbiturates.

Because barbiturates and benzodiazepines depress or slow down normal brain functioning, they may be useful in treating anxiety, sleep disorders, epilepsy, and other medical problems, as well as in inducing unconsciousness, as when they are used for anesthesia. This effect is sometimes called "gabaergic," referring to the increased inhibition that benzodiazepines or barbiturates superimpose on the central nervous system.[10]

If an individual develops a physical dependence on barbiturates or benzodiazepines, then he or she will experience withdrawal symptoms if the drug is suddenly stopped for any reason. Consequently, according to the National Institute on Drug Abuse (NIDA), the brain may then develop a rebound and suddenly speed up from its former more lethargic state, which may lead to seizures.[11]

Some research indicates that the GABA-benzodiazepine receptors in the nervous system, which interact with GABA, may be altered in patients who have anxiety disorders. For example, some studies have compared the effect of administering the benzodiazepine antagonist drug flumazenil to patients. This drug is sometimes used to reverse the effect of benzodiazepines, as when patients have overdosed on benzodiazepines. In studies of patients who have been diagnosed with panic disorder, the administration of fluma-zenil induced a panic attack, while it had no effect in patients without panic disorder. It may be true, thus, that individuals with anxiety disorders have a reduced level of GABA or they may have fewer GABA-benzodiazepine recep-tors.[12] As a result, these individuals may be more responsive to barbiturates or benzodiazepines.

There are major differences in the effects of barbiturates and benzodiaz-epines. For example, it is important to understand that although tolerance to a barbiturate develops with continued use, thus requiring greater amounts of the drug to achieve the same results, the upper limit of the drug that the body can tolerate does *not* increase. This is referred to as a narrow **therapeutic-to-toxic range.** Consequently, some individuals who are addicted to barbiturates cause their own accidental deaths by increasing their use of the drug.[13] This is not true in the case of benzodiazepines, however, and often dosages that are many times greater than the standard dose can be taken without causing death.[14] Of course, the excessive or long-term use of benzodiazepines is not recommended. However, some individuals take such drugs for many years.

BARBITURATES AND BENZODIAZEPINES DANGERS

Some categories of individuals should either altogether avoid barbiturates and benzodiazepines or use them only with caution. For example, elderly people and pregnant women should be very careful with these drugs for different reasons. These drugs may be dangerous for pregnant women because they may be harmful to the developing fetus. Older people may be very sensitive to the effects of barbiturates and benzodiazepines and in some older individuals these drugs may have a paradoxical excitatory action. As a result, this entire category of drugs is generally not recommended at all for older individuals. Barbiturates are also on several lists of drugs to be avoided in the elderly, such as a list that is provided to physicians and others by the National Commit-tee for Quality Assurance in the United States.[15] The key reason for avoiding these drugs in the elderly is that they are addictive and can lead to confusion and sedation.[16]

In a study by Robert C. Abrams, M.D., on fatal overdoses in New York City during the period 1990 to 2006, 27.2 percent of adults age 60 years and older who overdosed on drugs used barbiturates. This was more than twice the rate for younger individuals who experienced fatal overdoses in the same time frame, or 11.8 percent for those between the ages of 18 and 59 years.[17]

Barbiturates interact with many other drugs, increasing, decreasing, or otherwise changing their effects. As a result, since many older people take multiple drugs, this is yet another reason for them to avoid barbiturates whenever possible. For example, barbiturates may increase the metabolism of acetaminophen (Tylenol), which can both decrease its efficacy and also increase the possibility of liver damage, since the liver processes acetaminophen. If an elderly person is prescribed a barbiturate, a lower dose than is normally indicated for a younger person is generally used with the older person.

BARBITURATES AND BENZODIAZEPINES THAT SHOULD BE AVOIDED BY THE ELDERLY

According to the National Committee for Quality Assurance, some barbiturates and benzodiazepines should not be taken by the elderly. Most barbiturates should be avoided, according to this group, including amobarbital, butabarbital, mephobarbital, pentobarbital, phenobarbital, and secobarbital.

Among benzodiazepines, the following drugs should be avoided by the elderly: chlordiazepoxide (Librium), diazepam (Valium), flurazepam (Dalmane), and the combination drug amitriptyline/chlordiazepoxide (Limbitrol).[19,20] These drugs may increase the risk for falls among the elderly, resulting in fractures. Benzodiazepines may also be excluded from coverage by Medicare Part D prescription benefits. Other experts advise against the use of higher dosages of short-acting benzodiazepines in the elderly, such as avoiding more than 3 mg of lorazepam, more than 60 mg of oxazepam, more than 2 mg of alprazolam, more than 15 mg of temazepam, and more than 0.125 mg of triazolam. The reason: elderly people have an increased sensitivity to higher dosages of these drugs.[21]

Older people are not the only ones who should be careful about possible drug interactions when they are taking barbiturates. For example, women who take oral contraceptives may experience contraceptive failure—pregnancy— if they also take barbiturates. Barbiturates may also affect the metabolism of various types of drugs, including, but not limited to, drugs in the following categories: calcium channel blockers, corticosteroids, tricyclic antidepressants, and anti-blood clotting drugs, such as warfarin (Coumadin.) Barbiturates may also increase the blood concentration of drugs such as levothyroxine (thyroid hormone), antipsychotics, and anticonvulsant medications.[18]

BARBITURATES, SUICIDE, AND ACCIDENTAL DEATH

The cause of death in a barbiturate overdose is usually cardiovascular collapse and respiratory arrest, which means that the heart fails and the person cannot breathe.[22] A barbiturate overdose may also cause kidney failure.[23] In addition, barbiturates are sometimes used by individuals who want to die and seek help from others to achieve this result, as with assisted suicide. This may occur when individuals with terminal diseases seek death but feel unable to complete an act of suicide.

According to the Drug Abuse Warning Network (DAWN) in their report on emergency room visits, there were 9,877 nonmedical uses of barbiturates in 2007 (the latest data available as of this writing) out of 855,838 emergency room visits for nonmedical use of drugs. Thus abuse of barbiturates represented about 1 percent of the total.[24]

This information tallies with that which was reported in a 2007 issue of the *American Journal of Managed Care*, in which researchers reported that 1 percent of 1,235 substance-abusing subjects who were seen in an emergency room in 2004 were identified as barbiturate abusers. (The most commonly abused drug in this study was alcohol, which was abused by 67 percent of the subjects.)[25]

Of those individuals who used drugs to attempt suicide in 2007, according to data from the Drug Abuse Warning Network (DAWN), there were 1,663 emergency room visits of individuals who used barbiturates to attempt to take their lives, or less than 1 percent (0.8 percent).[26]

According to Medline Plus from the National Institutes of Health, of those individuals who overdose using barbiturates, either barbiturates alone or barbiturates combined with other drugs (including alcohol), the death rate is 10 percent, and it may be even higher if treatment is not received promptly by the individual.[27]

Accidental deaths do occur with the abuse of barbiturates. For example, in 1970, rock singer and guitarist Jimi Hendrix choked to death on his own vomit at the age of 27 after abusing barbiturates. Many other celebrities have died of barbiturate abuse, including Judy Garland and Marilyn Monroe as well as George Sanders, who committed suicide.

Sometimes it can be difficult or impossible to determine whether the death was an accident or a suicide. As stated in 1964 by the Committee on

PREGNANT WOMEN SHOULD AVOID BARBITURATES AND BENZODIAZEPINES

Women who are pregnant should avoid barbiturates or benzodiazepines altogether because the child could be born with an addiction to barbiturates and consequently will suffer from withdrawal symptoms as a newborn baby.[28] In addition, most barbiturates and benzodiazepines are designated as FDA Pregnancy Category D, which indicates a serious risk. Many drugs are designated as Pregnancy Category C, a more benign rating, in which the individual needs to exercise caution. The only worse category than Category D is Pregnancy Category X, in which the drug is absolutely contraindicated for use by pregnant women.

Some fetal risks that are directly associated with the pregnant woman's use of benzodiazepines may include cleft palate and cleft lip, intrauterine fetal death, and fetal growth restriction. According to physician Joan Keegan and her associates in their 2010 article on addiction in pregnancy, published in the *Journal of Addictive Diseases,* physicians also should consider the possible abuse of other drugs among women who use benzodiazepines, particularly considering the possible use of tobacco and alcohol. They also noted that benzodiazepines should not be abruptly stopped during pregnancy because of the extreme withdrawal symptoms that are often associated with the sudden ceasing of benzodiazepine use.[29]

LOW RISK OF SUBSTANCE DEPENDENCE FOR CNS DEPRESSANTS PRESCRIBED FOR EPILEPSY

In a study in Germany, published in 2009 in CNS *Neuroscience Therapy*, the researchers found that when barbiturates or the benzodiazepine clobazam (not approved for use in the United States) were used to treat patients with epilepsy, the risk for addiction was low. When they were withdrawn from their medication, about half the patients reported withdrawal symptoms yet less than 10 percent experienced any craving for the drug or a feeling of loss of control. The researchers reported that their study confirmed their hypothesis that barbiturates and benzodiazepines do not present a major problem of substance dependence among patients with epilepsy.[31]

Public Health of the New York Academy of Medicine in their article for the *Bulletin of the New York Academy of Medicine* on barbiturate deaths, and which is still true today:[30]

> Not all persons who die from misuse of barbiturates intend to kill themselves. Some have no thought of suicide but die from an accidental overdose of the drug. Then there is a second group of persons who threaten to kill themselves but do not really intend to die. Death comes when they miscalculate in the dosage or in their arrangements to be saved.

EMERGENCIES INVOLVING NONMEDICAL USE OF BENZODIAZEPINES

Excessive use of benzodiazepines or barbiturates as well as combining them with other drugs can and does lead to the need for emergency treatment in many cases. According to the Drug Abuse Warning Network (DAWN), in 2007 there were 217,640 emergency room visits involving benzodiazepines. Of specified drugs, the benzodiazepine drug causing the greatest problem was alprazolam (Xanax), followed by clonazepam (Klonopin). The nonmedical use of benzodiazepines leading to the need for emergency treatment

Table 3.1 Emergency Department Visits Involving Nonmedical Uses of Benzodiazepines, 2007		
Benzodiazepine	Number of Emergency Department Visits	Percent of All Emergency Department Visits Related to Nonmedical Use
All Benzodiazepines	218,640	26%
Alprazolam	80,313	9%
Clonazepam	40,920	5%
Diazepam	19,674	2%
Lorazepam	26,213	3%
Benzodiazepines, Not Otherwise Stated	55,346	7%

Source: Substance Abuse and Mental Health Services Administration, Office of Applied Studies. Drug Abuse Warning Network, 2007: National Estimates of Drug-Related Emergency Department Visits. National Institutes of Health: Rockville, Md., May 2010. Page 40.

increased from 143,546 visits in 2004 to 218,640 in 2007, a disturbing increase of 52 percent.[32] See the breakdown in Table 3.1 of the specific types of benzodiazepines involved in these emergency treatments.

In more recent data available from the Centers for Disease Control and Prevention (CDC), there were 271,700 nonmedical use emergency room visits in 2008. Among patients treated in emergency rooms who misused drugs, the most frequently appearing drug was alprazolam, which accounted for 104,800 visits. This was more than twice the amount of the next most abused benzodiazepine, or clonazepam (48,400 visits). According to the CDC, alprazolam was also the most prescribed benzodiazepine in 2008, with 44 million prescriptions written for the drug that year.[33]

WITHDRAWAL FROM BARBITURATES

In general, individuals who are withdrawing from barbiturates should **taper** down their dosage, under the careful control of a physician, rather than abruptly ending the usage of the drug.[34] Withdrawal symptoms will occur within about 12–20 hours after the last dosage of the drug, although they are

Table 3.2 Signs of Barbiturate Withdrawal	
Stage	Symptoms
Early Withdrawal	Increased pulse and/or blood pressure, anxiety, panic attacks, restlessness, and gastrointestinal upset.
Mid Withdrawal	Tremor, fever, diaphoresis, insomnia, anorexia, and diarrhea
Late Withdrawal	Changes in consciousness, profound agitation, hallucinations, autonomic instability, and seizures. **Patients showing signs of late withdrawal should seek prompt hospitalization.**

significantly milder when tapering occurs.[35] Psychotic behavior and hallucinations may also occur with sudden withdrawal from barbiturates.

After withdrawal symptoms start, they may occur over the next 8–36 hours, and withdrawal symptoms may also still be seen within up to seven days of the last use of the barbiturate. If the withdrawal is severe, the individual should be treated in the intensive care unit of the hospital, because he or she is a critical patient. Phenobarbital, a long-acting barbiturate, may be given to help a person withdraw from a shorter-acting barbiturate and to decrease the risk of seizures.[36]

Seizures resulting from withdrawal may occur from one to nearly five days after the drug use was ended, and more than one seizure usually occurs. In addition, patients may develop a psychosis that is similar to the delirium tremens suffered by individuals withdrawing from alcohol.[37] See Table 3.2 for further information on withdrawal symptoms from barbiturates.

BENZODIAZEPINES AND SUICIDE ATTEMPTS

Some individuals use benzodiazepines for the specific purpose of committing suicide while others die of an accidental overdose in the course of combining benzodiazepines with other drugs. It may be unclear whether the death was accidental or a suicide. According to the Drug Abuse Warning Network, however, there were 53,509 emergency room visits related to suicide attempts with the use of benzodiazepines in 2007, which represented nearly a third (27.2 percent) of all drugs that were used in suicide attempts related to emergency room visits. Of all suicide visits involving drugs, 9.7 percent involved alprazolam, followed by clonazepam (7.3 percent), lorazepam (4.8 percent), and diazepam (3.5 percent). There was a 45 percent increase in the number of suicide attempts using benzodiazepines from 2004 to 2007.[38]

In a study by the Centers for Disease Control and Prevention (CDC) of unintentional medication overdose deaths that occurred in Oklahoma for deaths over the period 1994–2006, the researchers identified 2,112 unintentional deaths. Most of the deaths occurred among males and those who were ages 35–54 years. Of the drugs that were involved in the unintentional deaths, alprazolam (Xanax) was present in 15 percent of the cases, the same percent as seen with accidental deaths from oxycodone. Other common drugs that caused unintentional deaths were methadone (31 percent) and hydrocodone (19 percent). The researchers

BENZODIAZEPINE OVERDOSES IN AUSTRALIA

In a study of drug overdoses in emergency departments at St. Vincent's Hospital in Melbourne, Australia, published in a 2010 issue of the *Australian and New Zealand Journal of Public Health,* researcher Penny Buykx and colleagues found that 77 percent of the drugs that were used in the overdose had been prescribed to the individuals for their treatment. Of concern was that benzodiazepines were most commonly used. Of 432 cases of medication misuse or overdose, benzodiazepines represented the largest category of drugs used, or 49 percent, followed by antidepressants, at the much lower rate of 19 percent. In addition, of the 213 cases of benzodiazepines used, diazepam (Valium) represented the most commonly used drug, or 46 incidents, followed by alprazolam (Xanax), at 26 incidents. Some individuals used more than one type of benzodiazepine.[41]

The researchers also found that most of the drugs had been prescribed to the individual who misused or overdosed on the drug. They also found that many of the individuals in the study had been taking benzodiazepines for long-term use. It is clear from this study that even among individuals who receive legitimate prescriptions, prescribing doctors need to exercise medical oversight and vigilance and also to consider whether the drug should be tapered and discontinued rather than used continuously for unspecified periods.

recommended that individuals ages 35–54 years should be warned ahead of time about the potential risks of misusing their prescription drugs.[39]

In another study of accidental deaths in West Virginia in 2006 and the contributing drugs to these deaths, the researchers identified 144 deaths caused by psychotherapeutic drugs such as benzodiazepines, antidepressants, and other psychotherapeutic drugs. Of these unintentional deaths, 66 individuals took diazepam (Valium) and 54 took alprazolam (Xanax). In less than half of the unintentional deaths in which diazepam was involved (45.5 percent), the drug was prescribed to the person who died, while in about two-thirds (64.8 percent) of the cases of individuals who died using alprazolam, the drug was prescribed to the individual. This indicates that greater physician oversight was likely needed. All those who died were also taking other prescription drugs and some were additionally taking illicit drugs and/or alcohol.[40]

DETOXIFICATION FROM THE EMERGENCY ROOM

According to the Drug Abuse Warning Network, about 14 percent of all emergency room visits in 2007 ended up in patients seeking **detoxification** (controlled withdrawal) services for benzodiazepine abuse. Of this 14 percent, alprazolam (Xanax) represented nearly half of the benzodiazepines of abuse (6.5 percent), followed by diazepam (Valium, 2.3 percent), clonazepam (Klonopin, 1.9 percent) and lorazepam (Ativan, 1.4 percent). Nonspecified benzodiazepines represented 3.4 percent of the cases. In contrast, barbiturates represent less than 1 percent of all drugs for which patients sought detoxification. In considering other drugs, the drug for which most patients sought detoxification was cocaine (46.5 percent), followed by heroin (30.2 percent) and marijuana (18.6 percent).[42]

OTHER DEPRESSANTS

In addition to the depressants categorized as barbiturates and benzodiazepines, other central nervous system depressants, including methaqualone (Quaalude), gamma hydroxybutyrate (GHB), and flunitrazepam (Rohypnol), can become drugs of abuse and dependence.

Methaqualone (Quaalude)

According to mental health professionals Roland R. Griffiths and Matthew W. Johnson, methaqualone is believed to bind to the GABA-A receptor site. It can be lethal in overdose. On a percentage score of the likelihood of abuse, the authors give it an 83 percent, a high score. In contrast, they give diazepam (Valium) a score of 67 percent and lorazepam a score of 57 percent.[43] The drug is banned in the United States because of its high addiction potential.

GHB

According to the National Institute on Drug Abuse (NIDA), GHB acts on the GABA-B receptor and another unnamed GHB binding site. When taken at high doses, GHB can cause sleep or coma or even death.[44]

In a focus group study with 51 individuals (30 men and 21 women), the subjects admittedly had abused GHB (mostly in liquid form and by the capful), and some individuals said they abused GHB daily. The average age of these individuals at their first reported use of the drug was 26.8 years, with a range of 13–50 years. According to researchers Judith C. Barker and colleagues, most participants stated their belief that GHB was not a particularly dangerous drug as long as the right dosage was taken. Yet despite their expressed concern for avoiding an overdose, few subjects said that they checked the dosage of the drug prior to using it. However, some reported that if they were at a party with their GHB-abusing friends, someone would write down the dosage of the GHB so they would not later forget how much of the drug was taken initially.[45]

Furthering the dangerousness of the drug ingestion, 80 percent said they took other drugs at the same time as their use of the GHB, such as alcohol, amphetamines, or marijuana. About half of the subjects said they mixed the GHB with other substances *before* taking it, such as mixing the dangerous stimulant methamphetamine with GHB. One mixture of drugs was referred to as EKG: Ecstasy, ketamine (a dissociative drug) and GHB.

These individuals obtained the drug from the Internet or from each other and some made their own GHB.

Flunitrazepam

Flunitrazepam acts on the GABA-A receptor and can cause amnesia while individuals are under the influence of the drug.[46] It is also known as a "date rape" drug.

4

How Barbiturates and Other Depressants Cause Addiction

Ted, 16, was at a party at his friend Gary's house, and was feeling kind of low. Gary's parents were out of town for the night, and they had put Gary in charge of the house. One of the first things Gary did was to invite all of his friends over for a party. Ted had to use the bathroom and while in there, on an impulse, he opened the medicine cabinet to see what was there. He noticed there were many prescription bottles although he didn't recognize any of the names. One drug, Ativan, had instructions on it to take one tablet per day. Ted felt pretty down, so he decided that if one pill was good, then three or four pills would be even better. So he grabbed a handful and swallowed them down with a glass of water. After he emerged from the bathroom, a friend handed him a drink that he said the guys had just invented, which had a major kick to it. Ted drank it all down.

Later that evening, Ted's friends thought he had fallen asleep but then they got scared because no one could wake him up. They didn't want to get in trouble so they carried Ted to the car and dropped him off at the emergency room. One of the girls tried to hide her face as she helped another boy drag Ted in and they told a nurse standing by that Ted was sick and couldn't wake up. Then they ran away. At first the nurse thought this was another stupid drunk kid who had passed out, but something didn't seem right. They checked further, and the emergency staff discovered that this was a case of an accidental drug overdose. The drugs Ted had taken were depressants, as was the strong alcoholic drink. The medical staff purposely put Ted into a deep coma-like sleep to help him recover.

ABUSIVE USES OF BARBITURATES

Although they are usually not the first choice of drugs of abuse among younger drug abusers (who are much more likely to abuse painkillers such as oxycodone or hydrocodone, or amphetamines, or marijuana), some younger individuals do abuse barbiturates, such as adolescents who raid the medicine cabinets of family members for drugs or others seeking sedating drugs (or sometimes seeking any drugs, whatever is available at the time, in a sort of Russian Roulette of drugs).

In a study of the abuse of prescription pain relievers by adolescents ages 12–17 years old, reported in 2008 in *Drug and Alcohol Dependence,* the most frequently abused drugs by adolescents were narcotics, including such drugs as Vicodin, Lortab, or Lorcet, and 52.3 percent of the nearly 2,000 adolescent subjects reported ever using these drugs in their lifetime. With regard to the barbiturates Fiornal and Fioricet, only 1.4 percent reported ever using these drugs, with a greater percentage of female users (2.1 percent) than male users (0.5 percent).[1] Of course, any level of abuse is problematic for those individuals who abuse drugs as well as for their family members.

HOW BENZODIAZEPINE (OR BARBITURATE) ABUSE BEGINS

According to psychiatrist Charles P. O'Brien in his article for the *Journal of Clinical Psychiatry,* some people begin to abuse benzodiazepines in one of two ways: either purposeful abuse or accidental abuse. For example, in the case of purposeful abuse, such individuals are already abusers of other drugs and they knowingly and willingly abuse a benzodiazepine (or barbiturate) to attain a high, as with heroin addicts who cannot obtain heroin and so instead they take methadone and then subsequently take a benzodiazepine such as diazepam (Valium) about two hours later to make the euphoria caused by the methadone last even longer. Another group of purposeful drug abusers are those who use benzodiazepines illicitly to help them come down from the euphoric high of stimulants such as cocaine or methamphetamine, often so that they can get some sleep.[3]

Others may be prescribed the drug by a doctor for anxiety, chronic headaches, or other problems. They later may find that they have developed a tolerance to the drug, needing a higher dosage to achieve the same effects. They

BARBITURATES COMBINED WITH ALCOHOL

Barbiturates are dangerous drugs when they are not used as directed by a physician, particularly since many abusers combine barbiturates

(*continues*)

Figure 4.1 Many abusers combine barbiturates with other sedating drugs, such as alcohol. (© *shutterstock*)

(continued)

with other sedating drugs, such as opiates or alcohol. As a result, such individuals may suffer from barbiturate intoxication, a condition in which the individual exhibits such symptoms as staggering, slurred speech, trouble thinking, shallow breathing, and slowed speech.

These symptoms often closely resemble the symptoms of alcohol intoxication, and it may be difficult or impossible for many people to distinguish the symptoms of barbiturate intoxication from alcohol intoxication, although a blood-alcohol test may reveal no alcohol or a low level of alcohol if the individual has not consumed any or little alcohol. If the symptoms of barbiturate intoxication become marked, the individual is in danger of death, and according to the National Institutes of Health (NIH), there is a 10 percent death rate from barbiturate overdose or barbiturate mixture overdose.[2]

may ask the doctor for more drugs, which is likely to trigger concern by the physician, who may decide that the patient needs to be treated for dependence. Conversely, those with a tolerance initially induced through prescription use may begin to exhibit drug-seeking behaviors, such as "**doctor shopping**" (seeing multiple doctors who do not know about each other in order to obtain prescriptions for drugs of abuse), or they may obtain the drugs from friends, the Internet, or drug dealers for the purpose of misusing them. They may also steal prescription pads and forge prescriptions. All of these behaviors are very dangerous, because without a doctor monitoring their drug use, the risk for adverse effects is high.

CRITERIA FOR ABUSE OR DEPENDENCE

Individuals who are abusers or are addicted to barbiturates or benzodiazepines have certain behavioral patterns similar to those who are addicted to other substances, such as alcohol, cocaine, amphetamines, and other drugs. The first criterion for substance abuse, for example, is a maladaptive pattern of use which impairs the person so that he or she fails at one or more important life obligations, such as going to work or school and performing competently

WITHDRAWAL FROM A MASSIVE ILLICIT DOSAGE OF FIORICET

Sometimes an addiction to one barbiturate can be treated with another barbiturate. An article in the *Archives of Neurology* in 2004 provides a disturbing description of a 37-year-old woman who was admitted to the hospital after suffering from initially unexplained grand mal seizures. Several years before this time, the patient had received a prescription from a physician for the drug Fioricet, a medication that combines the barbiturate butalbital with codeine and acetaminophen. The drug had been prescribed to the patient for headaches. But then the patient (who stopped seeing the doctor, when he refused to give her as many pills as she wanted) began purchasing the drug over the Internet, taking up to 20 tablets a day for a period of three months. The patient told the emergency room doctors that she had purchased up to 500 pills of Fioricet in one order with no problem.

When she stopped taking the drug, she developed agitation, tachycardia (dangerously rapid heartbeat), visual hallucinations, and seizures. In the emergency room, benzodiazepines, antipsychotics, and other barbiturates were administered but to no effect. The patient became severely distressed and she tried to climb over the side of the hospital bed rails. She was then treated with intravenous midazolam, a barbiturate, and that drug sedated her sufficiently. The patient's treatment was continued with phenobarbital, a long-acting barbiturate, and she was slowly tapered off the phenobarbital.[4]

or providing for the care of one's own children. Another criterion for abuse is that the person abuses the substances and then performs dangerous activities, such as driving a car or operating a dangerous machine. Experiencing frequent legal issues, such as getting arrested for public intoxication or disorderly conduct, is another criterion. In addition, the person who abuses substances often has confrontations with others about his or her substance abuse, such as verbal or even physical arguments with others.

If a person is dependent on drugs or other substances, the person usually exhibits a tolerance, or a need for increasingly greater amounts of the drug to achieve the same effects. (Tolerance alone is not sufficient to constitute addiction, since patients taking opioids for severe pain may develop a tolerance to the drug.) The addict spends a great deal of time obtaining the drug, using it, and then recovering from its effects. The addicted person also may give up activities or hobbies that were formerly important. The addict continues to take the drug even when he or she knows that it causes a physical and/or psychological problem for them.

PRIMARY USERS AND ABUSERS OF BENZODIAZEPINES

Benzodiazepines are used legitimately by individuals suffering from anxiety disorders and insomnia as well as epilepsy, and women outnumber men in the use of most benzodiazepines. According to Anna T. Theodorou and colleagues in their 2009 article for the *American Journal of Pharmacy Benefits,* in their retrospective study of antianxiety medications prescribed in 2008–2009, which was drawn from millions of prescriptions from the CVS Caremark database, the researchers found that 63 percent of the patients who were prescribed benzodiazepine drugs were female, and most of the subjects were ages 41–50 years old. However, in considering specific generations or large groups of people, Baby Boomers (ages 44–62 years in 2009) represented the largest group of individuals with benzodiazepine prescriptions, or 43 percent, followed by Generation X (ages 30–43 years), with 23 percent of the total benzodiazepine prescriptions.[5]

Abusers are often individuals who take the drugs to come down from a high that was induced by amphetamines or other stimulants that were abused, sometimes so they can get some sleep. However, elderly individuals may also become dependent on benzodiazepines. Risk factors for such dependence among the elderly are persistent pain and isolation, as well as the use of multiple medications and the presence of both depression and alcoholism. Some research indicates that benzodiazepine abuse is less likely to be recognized by physicians when it occurs among older women.

This is problematic because, as noted in a 2010 article for the *American Journal on Addictions,* dependence on benzodiazepines can develop into depression, anxiety, and even dementia.[6] The abuse or misuse of benzodiazepines

ILLICIT BENZODIAZEPINES PURCHASED ONLINE

Purchasing benzodiazepines over the Internet is associated with increased risk for the user, whose usage is not medically supervised. In one case, a 62-year-old patient was initially given lorazepam (Ativan) for insomnia by his physician. The drug was discontinued but the patient later presented to the emergency room with a panic attack and was prescribed alprazolam (Xanax). He was also prescribed temazepam (Restoril), another benzodiazepine drug. In addition, the patient's family purchased alprazolam for the patient on the Internet; thus he was taking three different benzodiazepines, including Ativan, Xanax, and Restoril.

This patient subsequently presented to the emergency room and was diagnosed with benzodiazepine dependence. The patient was treated with diazepam (Valium) to help him taper off the three other benzodiazepines. However, within 36 hours, he became extremely agitated and fearful and stabbed himself in the stomach, requiring emergency surgery. The patient was also stabilized on diazepam but he failed to comply with his physician's instructions, and continued to take other benzodiazepines, later being admitted to the intensive care unit for severe self-inflicted wounds to the neck and chest. The doctors noted that benzodiazepine dependence can develop quickly and it is also important to ascertain the extent of the benzodiazepine usage as accurately as possible.

It is highly unlikely that any of the physicians involved with this patient had any suspicions that he was abusing benzodiazepines that were purchased over the Internet along with the benzodiazepines that were actually prescribed to him.[8]

can also complicate the diagnosis of symptoms in an older person; for example, causing the clinician to assume the patient has a dementia associated with older age rather than symptoms caused by drugs. A urine drug screen can detect the presence of drugs such as benzodiazepines.

Some researchers have found that elderly people living in the community and who may be dependent on benzodiazepines can be effectively screened with two questions, including as follows:

1. Over the past 12 months, have you noticed any decrease in the effect of this medication? Yes/No
2. Have you tried to stop taking this medication? Yes/No

Individuals who respond "yes" to both questions are very likely to be addicted to benzodiazepines and they need treatment.[7]

If the patient is withdrawn from benzodiazepines suddenly then the patient can develop agitation and seizures. This can sometimes happen with hospitalization if the patient fails to inform the hospital of all drugs taken.

THREE TYPES OF BENZODIAZEPINE-DEPENDENT INDIVIDUALS

According to a study published in the journal *Current Opinion in Psychiatry* in 2005, there are three major types of individuals who are dependent on benzodiazepines. First are those individuals who are taking a therapeutic dosage of benzodiazepines and who have been taking the drug long-term for months or years. At least half of this population is dependent on the drug, and many are older female patients. Others in this category include individuals with psychiatric and physical problems as well as those who are elderly patients living in institutions.[9] Note that most experts do not regard such use as addiction unless there is also drug-seeking behavior and a craving for the drug, and they do not consider a physical tolerance alone as sufficient to consider the patient as drug dependent.

The second type of individuals who are addicted to benzodiazepines, according to this study, are those who were prescribed benzodiazepines and subsequently escalated their own dosages. At first, they may convince the doctor to increase the dosage, but once the doctor refuses to increase the dosage any further, they may exhibit doctor shopping behavior, obtaining prescriptions from multiple doctors. When these attempts fail, they may buy benzodiazepines illegally from drug dealers or online.[10]

The third category of individuals who become dependent on benzodiazepines are those who began their use of the drug by obtaining it illegally.

Many people in this category also abuse other drugs, such as amphetamines, cocaine, or alcohol. The benzodiazepines are used to potentiate the euphoria that other drugs give them or they take the drug to come down from an excessive high caused by other drugs. This 2005 study estimated at least 200,000 people fit this third category of benzodiazepine abusers in the United States.[11]

BENZODIAZEPINE ABUSE AND DEPENDENCE

When benzodiazepines are used on a chronic basis, the individual will develop a tolerance to the drug, and this is a concern for many psychiatrists. However, addiction is not inevitable, because other elements of drug dependence, such as drug seeking, craving, and the failure to perform at work or in school may not be met. Despite this, when other drugs can be used to treat the same condition, such as antidepressants, many experts prefer their use, since antidepressants are not addictive, nor are they scheduled as potentially dangerous drugs by the Drug Enforcement Administration.

It is also important to consider whether the drugs are used for the treatment of a specific condition while the individual is under the control of a physician or whether they are misused or abused; for example, the drug may be prescribed for a person who is severely anxious, a legitimate use.

Patients who take benzodiazepines as directed by their physician for an anxiety disorder, chronic insomnia, or another medical problem may develop a low-level tolerance. If they suddenly stop taking the medication for some reason, they may develop withdrawal symptoms. In general, high dosages should be avoided, even among those taking benzodiazepines under the control of a doctor.[12]

WITHDRAWAL FROM BENZODIAZEPINES

It is never advisable for a person who has been using benzodiazepines to suddenly stop taking these drugs. Instead, the drug should be tapered off so that the body can adjust to the lower levels of the drug in the system. A sudden withdrawal of the drug can lead to severe anxiety, insomnia, and even death. The reason for this is that with long-term use of benzodiazepines, the drug takes over many functions that were formerly linked to the natural GABA neurotransmitter system. As a result, when the drug is withdrawn, the person is in a state of GABA underactivity, which then causes the nervous system to experience a hyperexcitability until the body adjusts.[13]

Withdrawal symptoms from benzodiazepines generally peak at seven days. Not all individuals experience withdrawal symptoms and, for example, less than half of patients (43 percent) taking diazepam for eight months or longer will experience withdrawal.[14] Withdrawal symptoms may resemble symptoms of anxiety, such as restlessness, difficulty concentrating, fear, and tension. The individual may also feel dizzy and experience profuse sweating, headache, insomnia, lack of appetite, and tremor.

Symptoms that are not typical of anxiety but which may occur with the withdrawal from benzodiazepines may include a metallic taste in the mouth, photophobia (sensitivity to light), phonophobia (sensitivity to sound), and muscle aches and pain.

Benzodiazepine use is problematic if the person also abuses alcohol at the same time as using the benzodiazepine, because when the drugs are combined it can be very dangerous, since they are both depressants.

OTHER DEPRESSANTS

Some drugs, such as GHB, are linked to a propensity for high-risk behavior, while other depressants, such as paraldehyde, can cause a dependence that is similar to alcoholism.

GHB

In a study of 131 GHB abusers that was published in 2007, the researchers tested the association between the hospitalization of GHB abusers among 26 subjects who used GHB and compared their hospitalizations with their high-risk behaviors.[15] High-risk behaviors included such acts as driving a vehicle while under the influence of GHB; having sex while under the influence of GHB; using GHB when alone; taking GHB with either Ecstasy or MDMA; taking GHB with ketamine; taking GHB with alcohol; using GHB 20 or more times in their lives; using GHB to prevent withdrawal symptoms; ever using heroin; or using precursors or analogues of GHB.

The researchers reported that almost one-third of the subjects admitted to driving while under the influence of GHB and these subjects were greater than three times more likely to need to be hospitalized. They also found that

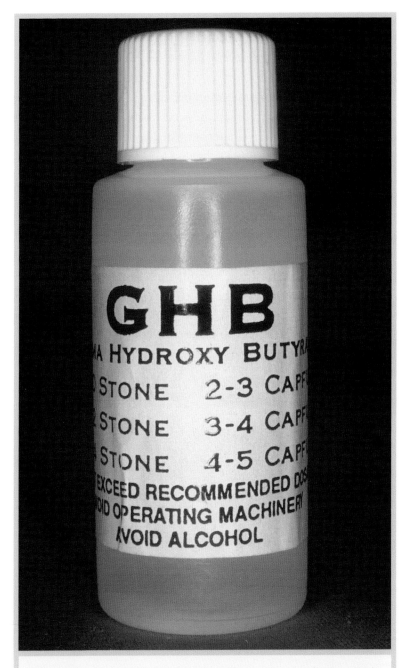

Figure 4.2 First synthesized in the 1920s as an anesthetic, GHB is an illegal drug in the United States today. Once used by body builders to bulk up muscle mass, the drug has also been used as a date rape drug. (© *David Hoffman Photo Library/ Alamy*)

those who were addicted to GHB and tried to withdraw from the drug had more than a three-times greater risk of hospitalization than the other subjects, and the researchers noted that several days of hospitalization may be needed to withdraw from GHB.

The greatest risk for hospitalization occurred among individuals engaging in multiple risk factors and these subjects had greater than ten times the risk of needing hospitalization when contrasted with GHB users who did not exhibit any high risk behaviors.

Paraldehyde

Frequent abuse of paraldehyde (Paral) can cause a physical dependence similar to alcohol dependence and individuals who are addicted will experience withdrawal if they stop using the drug.[16] Some individuals who have become addicted to alcohol used the drug during treatment; however, some switched their drug of addiction from alcohol to paraldehyde, defeating the purpose of drug treatment. Paraldehyde has a strong odor that is unpleasant to most people. It is a Schedule IV depressant.[17]

5

Addiction Treatment and Recovery

Lori, age 29, had an abuse problem with both benzodiazepines and cocaine. She abused cocaine solely for the euphoria that it induced in her. But sometimes she became far too exhausted from the cocaine high she experienced, and when that happened, which was occurring more and more frequently, she just wanted to come down from the euphoria enough so that she could get some sleep. Those were the occasions when she took either alprazolam (Xanax) or sometimes some diazepam (Valium); whatever she could get her hands on. Lori obtained these drugs from friends or family members or sometimes she bought them on the street. Lori was starting to worry that she had a problem with cocaine. But she didn't realize she also had a problem with benzodiazepine drugs.

Recovery from abuse or dependence on barbiturates or benzodiazepines can be difficult for several reasons. First, many people who abuse these drugs also abuse other substances, such as alcohol, and thus they need treatment for all their addictions. This leads to another problem, which is that treatment facilities may be set up to treat alcohol dependence or addiction to another drug but not addictions to multiple substances. In addition, many clinics may have little knowledge of addictions to barbiturates or benzodiazepines, since they concentrate on clients with substance issues related to alcohol, cocaine, or amphetamine.

TREATMENT CENTERS

Centers for the treatment of substance dependence may be long-term facilities, short-term facilities, or outpatient facilities. According to NIDA, residential or outpatient treatment that lasts for less than 90 days is generally not effective because most people need a longer treatment period. NIDA reports that factors that are related to success with treatment include a strong motivation to change drug-using behavior; the support of the family and friends; and sometimes pressure from law enforcement, employers, and the child protection system.[1]

SUPPORT GROUPS

Self-help organizations can be enormously helpful to individuals, and Narcotics Anonymous is an organization that has helped individuals worldwide with their addiction to drugs of all sorts. There are no dues and individuals can attend meetings in most cities in the world. The goal is abstinence from the drug of abuse, and fellow addicts provide help and support. A sponsor is assigned who assists the individual when he or she feels at risk for abusing the drug. Individuals work through the 12 steps associated with the group, based on the 12 steps of Alcoholics Anonymous and adapted for Narcotics Anonymous. The first step is to recognize and acknowledge to yourself that you are helpless to solve your addiction on your own. Other steps lead individuals through the recovery process.

KEY ISSUES WITH TREATMENT OF ABUSE OR DEPENDENCE

In general, there are two key issues associated with treating the abuse or dependence to barbiturates or benzodiazepines. First, tapering off of the drug is almost always necessary to avoid severe complications. A sudden withdrawal from some depressant drugs can cause symptoms that are even more severe than are found with the withdrawal from heroin or alcohol and they can also be fatal. This is particularly true with the case of withdrawal from alprazolam (Xanax). Next, medications are sometimes used to help with the withdrawal and sometimes a long-acting drug in the same class may be used for withdrawal from a barbiturate or benzodiazepine.

TAPERING OFF THE BARBITURATE OR BENZODIAZEPINE

It is best to taper off drugs such as barbiturates or benzodiazepines, to avoid severe withdrawal symptoms. In their article on withdrawing from benzodiazepines, Dr. M. Lader and colleagues emphasized the importance of tapering, but also stated that tapering should not exceed a time frame of more than six months because if tapering lasts longer than this period, then withdrawal can become the focus of the patient's entire existence.[2] It was known as far back as 1983 that individuals who abused or were dependent on benzodiazepines

PREDICTORS FOR SUCCESS WITH BENZODIAZEPINE ABSTINENCE

In a study of 180 patients in the Netherlands who were dependent on benzodiazepine, one group received tapering and group therapy and saw their physician weekly for six weeks. Individuals in this group were given an equivalent dosage of diazepam to the benzodiazepine to which they were addicted for two weeks and then were tapered off the drug by 25 percent each week. They also received five sessions of group therapy during the tapering off period. The patients in the control group did not receive any attention regarding their benzodiazepine usage. Subjects in the study were an average age of 63 years and 70 percent were women. Benzodiazepines had been used for an average of 13.5 years prior to the study. The patients were then followed and 170 were successfully contacted. About one-third (29 percent) had successfully maintained benzodiazepine abstinence.[6]

Some key predictors of success were as follows: being in a program that tapered the patient off benzodiazepines and which also offered group therapy, making a substantial reduction in benzodiazepine usage by the patients themselves before they began tapering off the drug, and having no use of alcohol. The group therapy was based on cognitive-behavioral therapy and also offered relaxation exercises and assistance with awareness of issues related to withdrawal as well as relapse.

should be tapered off the drug. Tapering off the drug will also help physicians to determine if the anxiety that develops is more likely to stem from an anxiety disorder or from withdrawal from the drug.

John Marks wrote that a gradual withdrawal of benzodiazepines should be used in those individuals who have been taking benzodiazepines for at least three continuous months, and he also noted that tapering was especially important if patients on benzodiazepines had been taking dosages above the normal therapeutic levels. Marks also noted that in most cases, benzodiazepine abuse or dependence also occurs along with other substance abuse or dependence.[3]

Some physicians use drugs to help patients withdraw from barbiturates or benzodiazepines. For example, phenobarbital, a barbiturate drug, may be used to help patients withdrawing from barbiturate dependence.[4]

With regard to dependence on benzodiazepine drugs, experts report that diazepam (Valium) may be used to taper off such benzodiazepines as alprazolam (Xanax), chlordiazepoxide (Librium), lorazepam (Ativan), nitrazepam (Mogadon), oxazepam (Serapax), and temazepam (Restoril). According to Dr. Eric Khong and colleagues, 10 mg of diazepam is approximately equal to the following amounts of other benzodiazepine drugs: 1 mg of alprazolam, 20 mg of chlordizepoxide, 1 mg of lorazepam, 10 mg of nitrazepam, 30 mg of oxazepam, and 20 mg of temazepam.[5]

STAGES OF CHANGE

Many people who abuse drugs of all types go through several basic stages of change. The University of Rhode Island Change Assessment Model describes four stages of change, including precontemplation, contemplation, action, and maintenance.[7] In the precontemplation stage, the person does not think that there is any problem with his or her drug use, and thus believes that there are no reasons to make any changes. Therapy may be ineffective at this stage, although the person may have been compelled by others or even by the court to attend therapy sessions.

In the contemplation stage, the person with substance abuse issues realizes there is a problem and is considering making changes, but is often not sure what to do or how to do it, and thus, may be openly receptive to following suggestions from therapists. In the action stage, the person is actively working on making changes, such as giving up drugs, starting or continuing therapy, and taking whatever other actions may be useful to "saying no" to drugs of abuse. Last, in the maintenance stage, the person has already made effective changes, and is no longer using drugs. However, there is still the risk of relapse and the person must actively work against falling back into the use of drugs, especially should life circumstances become more difficult, as often happens.

PSYCHOLOGICAL THERAPIES

The most frequently used and successful psychological therapies for substance abuse in the 21st century are cognitive-behavioral therapy and brief intervention therapy. According to the National Institute of Mental Health (NIMH), cognitive-behavioral therapy (CBT) teaches an individual to learn to identify internal thoughts they may have which prevent them from acting in their own best interests and then learn to replace these problem thoughts with more realistic and helpful ones.[8]

Brief intervention therapy refers to the doctor or therapist telling the patient that his or her use of the drug is problematic and pointing out to the patient what is the likely outcome if the drug is continued at the current level (such as getting fired from a job, his or her partner leaving, and so forth).

Motivational interviewing is another form of therapy used to treat drug abuse and dependence. In addition, progressive muscle relaxation is a technique that can help individuals who abuse or are addicted to drugs to deal with the stress in their lives and be more receptive to therapeutic techniques.

In concert with receiving therapy, substance abusers often must make other lifestyle changes, such as ending associations with friends or relatives who continue to abuse drugs. In addition, therapists help former abusers reclaim past interests and develop new healthy interests, to replace their former concentration on abusing drugs.

Cognitive-Behavioral Therapy

With CBT, the therapist helps the individual to identify thinking patterns that are maladaptive or destructive and that lead to drug use, and then teaches the individual to challenge these particular thoughts. For example, one thought that may present to individuals addicted to many different substances is, "My life is terrible. I need some ___ (type of barbiturate, benzodiazepine or other drug)." The person's life may in fact really *not* be going well, but the reality is that drugs that are used for abuse cannot change the course of his or her life in a positive way. Instead, abused drugs will keep the person on the same path or in a negative downward spiral. Thus, the thought can be changed to "My life is not going well at all. I need to make changes that don't involve drugs." The "old" thoughts will often recur and may feel very powerful and urgent, but the individual can learn to challenge these thoughts internally and resist them. Eventually, the new thought patterns will dominate and old thoughts will decrease.

CBT can be used both in individual sessions as well as in group ther apy with a leader. According to the Substance Abuse and Mental Health Services Administration, two-thirds of substance abuse treatment facilities use CBT always or often, while 25 percent report using this form of therapy

Figure 5.1 Cognitive-behavioral therapy, one treatment for those with a substance abuse problem, teaches individuals to identify thoughts they may have which prevent them from acting in their own best interests, and then learn to replace these problem thoughts with more realistic and helpful ones. (© David Grossman/ Photo Researchers Inc.)

sometimes.[9] CBT is also used to treat addiction to drugs when an individual has a relapse. In fact, relapses are common among drug abusers. Facilities that treat addiction often offer relapse prevention therapy, and the Substance Abuse and Mental Health Services Administration reports that relapse prevention is used always or often by 87 percent of treatment facilities.[10] The National Institute of Mental Health (NIMH) notes that both the therapist and the patient must be actively engaged and involved with CBT.[11] It is an interactive process for the parties involved.

Brief Intervention Therapy

Brief intervention therapy is often surprisingly effective. There are generally from one to five sessions of brief intervention when this type of therapy is used, according to the Substance Abuse and Mental Health Services Administration, and about one-third (35 percent) of treatment facilities use this form of therapy always or often, while 45 percent report relying upon it sometimes.[12]

Motivational Interviewing

Motivational interviewing is a form of nonconfrontational type of therapy that is used with individuals who are uncertain about whether they can or want to make changes in their lives. Those who support this form of therapy believe that this ambivalence about making changes is a key barrier and thus enhancing the desire to change will lead to the ability to make changes. The goal with this form of therapy is to enhance the individual's desire to make changes to his or her life, such as giving up drugs. According to the Substance Abuse and Mental Health Services Administration, more than half (55 percent) of all treatment facilities use MI always or often while 30 percent use it sometimes.[13] Motivational interviewing can be used with both individual and group therapy.

Combining Psychotherapies

Some therapists use a combination of types of psychotherapy. In a study in Germany of individuals addicted to prescription drugs, including sedatives, opiates, and other drugs, the researchers studied 126 patients. The study group received two counseling sessions, which were regarded as a brief intervention form of therapy, and the sessions were based on motivational interviewing. The control group was given a booklet on health behavior. After three months, about 18 percent of the study group discontinued their use of the drugs, compared to about 9 percent of the control group, thus, the study group was twice as successful as the control group. In addition, about 52 percent of the study group reduced their drug use, compared to 30 percent of the control group.[14] Clearly, several sessions of motivational interviewing in a brief intervention was effective at reducing problem drug use.

Progressive Muscle Relaxation

Dr. Khong and colleagues recommend that individuals withdrawing from benzodiazepines use progressive muscle relaxation therapy to manage their stress and insomnia. Progressive muscle relaxation is a technique in which the person is trained to tighten one muscle group and then completely relax that area. Before starting, the person should breathe slowly and deeply. Dr. Khong and his colleagues recommend starting with the face and moving to the shoulders and then the back, stomach, pelvic area, the legs and feet, and last, the toes. The tensed muscles should be held for 15 seconds than relaxed for 30 seconds before the person moves to the next part of the body. It's also recommended that after the progressive muscle relaxation, the person should breathe slowly and deeply and relax for about a minute or so.[15]

Lifestyle Changes

People who abuse barbiturates or benzodiazepines may associate with others who are also abusers and these friends may also abuse these drugs as well. In fact, therapies such as CBT help patients identify situations in which they are

INVOLUNTARY TREATMENT WORKS

According to the National Institute of Drug Abuse (NIDA), individuals who go into drug treatment under the duress of legal pressure have outcomes that are as favorable as individuals who enter treatment voluntarily.[16] This means that, for example, if a court compels treatment, the individual has as good a chance for recovering from drugs as those who choose to enter treatment.

likely to abuse drugs or to wish to abuse drugs. As a result, therapists may encourage drug abusers to break away from friends and even family members who continue to abuse drugs and who fail to accept that they have a problem. It can be very hard to maintain a new healthy lifestyle when others important in one's life are using drugs and encouraging the individual to go back to drug abuse. Therapists can teach individuals how to avoid old friends, associates, and even family members who persist in drug abuse and to develop new and healthy relationships.

Therapists can also encourage former drug abusers to return to past interests that they have long neglected, such as tinkering with cars, collecting toy trains, or running marathon races. In addition, therapy can help individuals develop new interests in music, art, or other areas, to heal the mind and the body.

6

Barbiturates, Other Depressants, and the Law

Larry, age 39, was in jail for not paying his child support. He gave the guards his Xanax pills when he was processed in, and they promised to give him his medication, but they never did. After a couple of days of feeling very anxious and increasingly sick, Larry started hallucinating, thinking that everyone was after him, although no one was really bothering him. Then he started frothing at the mouth and having seizures. The guards said he was just faking it. On the sixth day of his imprisonment, Larry fell down and he lost consciousness. He died shortly thereafter.

Larry's family sued the prison for wrongful death and they won several million dollars, although the suit was bitterly contested by the prosecutor. After Larry's death, the prison looked into whether it was still okay to withhold benzodiazepines from inmates who said that they took them, after it was verified with the prescribing doctor that these inmates really did have prescriptions for the drug. They decided that it was not an acceptable practice and changed their former policy against ignoring patients who said they took psychiatric drugs under the treatment of a physician.

The Drug Enforcement Administration divides drugs into five schedules, with Schedule I including illegal drugs and Schedule II including drugs that have a high potential for addiction and abuse. Schedules III and IV supposedly have a lower potential for abuse or dependence, and Schedule V has the least potential for abuse or addiction. Most barbiturates are Schedule II or III drugs, while most benzodiazepines are Schedule IV drugs. This does not, however, mean that benzodiazepines are necessarily safer than barbiturates. People can and sometimes do overdose and sometimes die because of an excessive use or abuse of benzodiazepines. In addition, individuals may abuse these central nervous system depressants in concert with other depressants, particularly alcohol.

ABUSED BENZODIAZEPINES

The National Forensic Laboratory Information System of the Drug Enforcement Administration reports on prescribed drugs that are diverted from lawful prescriptions, and a study that was reported in late 2006 indicated that diazepam (Valium) and alprazolam (Xanax) were the leading drugs of diversion among benzodiazepines. The diversion rate of alprazolam was estimated at about 19 percent in 2005, up from 15 percent in 2001. The diversion rate for diazepam, however, was a little lower in 2005 (11 percent) than it was in 2001 (14 percent).[1]

According to the Drug Enforcement Administration, in the first six months of 2010, the following units of tablets or capsules were submitted to local, state, and federal forensic laboratories as diverted drugs: 16,816 alprazolam; 4,191 clonazepam; 2,840 diazepam; 889 lorazepam; and 146 temazepam.[2]

SUBSTANCE ABUSE AMONG PRISON INMATES

According to the Federal Bureau of Prisons, up to 35 percent of inmates who are incarcerated in local jails nationwide in the United States were under the influence of drugs when they committed their offense. The drug might have been alcohol or other depressants or it could have been stimulants. Many criminals use a combination of drugs before committing their crimes. Prison officials need to perform a substance abuse assessment of new inmates because their withdrawal from alcohol, sedatives, or anxiolytics (benzodiazepines) can be very dangerous and even life threatening for the individual.[3]

The person might be a drug dealer or may have committed another serious crime, but many people would agree that he or she should not be given, in effect, the death penalty by withholding drugs from an addicted individual. Instead, treatment should continue. However, this is an extremely controversial issue among prison officials, who are highly aware of the presence of

PRISON WASTEWATER AND XANAX ABUSE

In a unique study in Spain in which researchers analyzed the prison wastewater for the presence of drugs of abuse by prisoners (or anyone else in the prison who was using the sewage system), the researchers found that the second most abused drug was alprazolam (Xanax), at a rate of 129 doses per day per 1,000 inhabitants of the prison. Methadone was the most abused drug, at 156 doses per day per 1,000 inhabitants. Other drugs of abuse were cannabis (33 doses per day per 1,000 inhabitants) and cocaine (3 doses per day per 1,000 inhabitants). Surprisingly, the test also revealed that there was only sporadic usage of such drugs as amphetamine, methamphetamine, and heroin, all drugs that many people may believe would be commonly abused in prison.[4]

Clearly alprazolam is a major drug of abuse among the prison population considered in this study. It would be interesting to discover if similar results were found in prisons in the United States. The researchers also found particular days in which drugs were most commonly used; for example, on July 15th, the consumption of the drugs alprozolam, methadone, heroin, and LSD spiked. The researchers noted that the staff could investigate whether special circumstances occurred on that day leading to a higher level of drug consumption.

illegal drugs in prisons and who also worry that by treating inmates with psychiatric drugs, then rates of drug abuse and diversion will increase further.

OBTAINING MISUSED DRUGS

Some people wonder how individuals obtain drugs that they abuse illicitly, and the answer is that there are many ways to do so. For example, some individuals rely on doctor shopping, receiving prescriptions which they subsequently fill at various different pharmacies, for which they pay in cash. Some doctors run "pill mills," offices where they will write prescriptions for nearly whatever drugs patients want and in large quantities. This practice, however, puts the doctor in danger of losing his or her medical license to practice.

Other individuals purchase their drugs over the Internet on illicit Web sites, which offer scheduled drugs for sale. These Web sites are often shut down by the Drug Enforcement Administration but others spring up in their place, because drug selling is highly profitable. If alerted by the DEA, credit card companies will refuse to allow customers to use their credit cards to make payments for the drugs on such Web sites.

Some people obtain benzodiazepines, barbiturates, or other drugs from their friends and relatives, and others steal the drugs from the medicine cabinets of their friends and relatives. Some individuals steal prescription pads from doctors and then write themselves prescriptions for the prescribed drugs that they want. Others forge prescriptions; for example, if the doctor orders one refill of a drug, then a patient may change the "1" to a "4." This is not possible with a Schedule II narcotic, because refills may not be ordered for drugs in this schedule. However, it is possible with benzodiazepines, which are Schedule IV drugs for which refills may be ordered by the doctor.

Some people make their own illicit drugs, as with the production of GHB. This drug is illegal to purchase in the United States and may only be manufactured and/or sold in violation of federal law.

DRUG TESTING FOR BARBITURATES AND BENZODIAZEPINES

Many organizations currently require drug testing, whether an individual is an applicant for a new job, a high school or college athlete, someone enlisting in the military, or a person in many other walks of life. In addition, law enforcement authorities such as the police and probation and parole departments frequently use drug testing to identify factors related to the commission of a crime as well as to identify whether a person on probation or parole is in violation because of illicit drug abuse. A positive drug test is nearly always a violation of probation or parole, which means that the person is at risk for being incarcerated, depending on the individual circumstances.

When the federal government requires drug testing, testing is always required for barbiturates and benzodiazepines, as well as for other substances. Of course, if an individual has a prescription for the drug, then this use is not illicit and should not present a problem to the individual.

Most drug testing is done with a urine sample, but barbiturates and benzodiazepines can also be tested for in samples of blood, saliva, or hair. If a person who must take a drug test has a legitimate prescription for a barbiturate or benzodiazepine medication, then he or she should take the prescription bottle to the test and show it to the examiner. In some cases, individuals may receive a false positive test for a barbiturate or benzodiazepine and in such cases they should request that a second confirming test be performed.

OTHER DEPRESSANTS

Several other depressants are of particular interest to law enforcement officials, such as gamma hydroxybutyrate (GHB) and flunitrazepam (Rohypol).

AVOIDING THE CONSUMPTION OF DATE RAPE DRUGS

According to the Office on Women's Health of the U.S. Department of Health and Human Services, individuals can protect themselves from a substance being placed in their drink for the purposes of sexual assault by following these guidelines:

- Do not accept drinks from others
- Open your own containers
- Keep your drink with you, even if you need to go to the bathroom
- Do not drink from punch bowls or other common containers
- If someone offers to get you a drink at a party or a bar, go with the person to order your own drink, watch it being poured or mixed, and then carry it yourself
- Do not drink anything that tastes or smells strange. GHB may taste salty
- If you realize that your drink was unattended, pour it out
- If you feel intoxicated but have not consumed alcohol or if the effects of alcohol feel stronger than usual, get help immediately.[8]

GHB

In studies of drug-facilitated sexual assault, when GHB was tested for, the drug was found in only about 4 percent of the cases if GHB was the only drug administered. However, the blood and urine samples were analyzed within about 72 hours of the assault, when the GHB could have already been metabolized by the body and thus have become undetectable. This is another reason why predators prefer GHB—by the time the victim realizes she or he may have been assaulted and seeks medical attention, the drug may no longer be detectable, and thus, the evidence is lost.[5]

Flunitrazepam (Rohypnol)

Flunitrazepam is a benzodiazepine and a very dangerous drug of interest to police and other law enforcement officials. The Drug-Induced Rape Prevention and Punishment Act of 1996 was passed as a direct result of the sexual misuse of this drug.[6]

According to the Office on Women's Health, flunitrazepam has been replaced as a date rape drug in some areas of the United States by benzodiazepines such as clonazepam (Klonopin) and alprazolam (Xanax).[7]

7
Summary

Barbiturates and benzodiazepines are central nervous system depressant drugs that have helped many people since the early to mid-20th century and beyond. For example, both types of drugs have helped people with anxiety and insomnia and both were initially used for many other disorders, such as depression, epilepsy, and other chronic medical problems. It is also true that barbiturates and benzodiazepines can be abused and misused.

Barbiturates have largely fallen out of favor as drugs of use or abuse and were essentially replaced by the entry of benzodiazepines into the drug arsenal of physicians. Today, however, some benzodiazepines are misused and abused, most prominently the drug alprazolam (Xanax), which is a frequent drug of abuse and dependence and is also the most frequently prescribed benzodiazepine drug as of this writing in 2011. Its use in patients should be carefully monitored by physicians, and patients should also be warned to never "share" their medication with others, because such an act is not only dangerous but it is also illegal.

It is yet unknown what will be the "next big thing" in popular medication categories that are used to treat anxiety disorders, insomnia, and the other conditions for which barbiturates and benzodiazepines have been used in the past and continue to be used by patients. However, in the present, sedating drugs such as nonbenzodiazepine gamma-aminobutyric acid receptor antagonists such as zaleplon (Sonata), zolpidem (Ambien), and eszopiclone (Lunesta) are used in either tablet or capsule form to treat short-term forms of insomnia. These are benzodiazepine-like central nervous system depressant drugs, and they are also Schedule IV scheduled drugs under the control of the Drug Enforcement Administration.[1]

Some experts postulate that creating novel forms for the administration of these drugs, such as the use of sublingual tablets or oral sprays, could be developed and that such a drug delivery would act more conveniently and quickly and also increase patient compliance with the prescribed drug regimen, although further studies are needed to determine if such forms would be sufficiently safe.[2]

There are already medications that are used to reverse the effect of benzodiazepines, and some experts recommend that the drug, flumazenil (Romazicon), perhaps could be used to treat individuals who are addicted to benzodiazepine drugs. Flumazenil is an injectable benzodiazepine antagonist that has been used to treat benzodiazepine overdoses. For example, several researchers in Australia created a form of a low dosage of flumazenil that was infused with a portable balloon infusion pump, using it to treat individuals who were dependent on benzodiazepines. Theoretically, this method could be effective at treating individuals with benzodiazepine dependence if it is approved by the Food and Drug Administration at a future point.[3]

In the initial studies that involved 13 people who were heavily dependent on benzodiazepines as well as other substances, the results of this form of drug delivery were very promising. For example in one case, a 32-year-old man received an infusion of flumazenil for eight months. This patient was a heavy drug abuser, and he had abused diazepam (Valium), oxazepam, (Serax), nitrazepam (Mogadon), and temazepam (Restoril) daily, as well as abusing methadone, heroin, amphetamines, and crack cocaine. This treatment patient reportedly had misused benzodiazepines to counteract the insomnia caused by the stimulants. Subsequent to treatment, follow-up revealed that the man stayed off benzodiazepines and all other drugs for two years. Other subjects had similar successes.[4]

Some studies indicate that the anticonvulsant pregabalin (Lyrica) is effective in treating both benzodiazepine dependence and alcohol dependence. This is important because individuals who are dependent on benzodiazepines may also have a problem with alcoholism, and thus pregabalin could theoretically help treat both problems. Pregabalin is an off-label treatment for benzodiazepine dependence and thus it is not approved by the FDA for this purpose as of this writing in 2011.

Greek psychiatrists Panagiotis Oulis and George Konstantakopoulos analyzed current studies on pregabalin used as a treatment for benzodiazepine and alcohol dependence, reporting their findings in 2010 in *CNS Neuroscience & Therapeutics*. They reported on a study of 15 patients who were dependent on benzodiazepines, including 12 women and three men, and who found improvement with treatment with pregabalin. In addition, the study results indicated that pregabalin may have an antidepressant effect as well as an anti-anxiety effect.[5]

It is unknown if pregabalin is effective at helping with withdrawal from barbiturate dependence and further studies could help ascertain its potential. However, since barbiturate abuse and dependence are both in a sharp decline compared to past years, such studies are unlikely to occur.

Although abstinence from addictive drugs is the gold standard for most addiction programs and for all 12-step support groups such as Narcotics Anonymous, some researchers report that some individuals, especially those taking high dosages of benzodiazepines and who find abstinence difficult or impossible, may be better served by being maintained on a long-acting benzodiazepine that has a slow onset. Swiss psychiatrist Michael Liebrenz and colleagues say the drug should be one that does not give an immediate feeling of euphoria, such as clonazepam (Klonopin) or other benzodiazepines. The advantages of such an approach would be that it could improve treatment compliance and retention by reducing craving and also decreasing anxiety, since benzodiazepines are antianxiety drugs. Disadvantages lie in patients who abuse alcohol because the combined effect of alcohol and any benzodiazepine can lead to a dangerous and even fatal level of sedation.[6] In addition, the maintenance usage of benzodiazepines may be problematic in that it could lead to a cognitive decline, particularly among elderly individuals.[7]

These experts suggest maintenance therapy for those who fit the following categories: individuals who abuse multiple types of benzodiazepines; those who escalate their dosage of the drug repeatedly; those who use benzodiazepines in order to potentiate the effects of other drugs; those who gain their benzodiazepines through illegal means; and those who have had negative social consequences as a result of their benzodiazepine abuse.[8]

Appendix: Criteria for Substance Abuse and Dependence

Individuals who abuse or are addicted to barbiturates, benzodiazepines, or other depressants have certain behavioral patterns similar to those who are addicted to other substances. The criteria for both substance abuse and dependence follow, as defined in the *Diagnostic and Statistical Manual of Mental Disorders, Fourth Edition (Text Revision)*, published by the American Psychiatric Association.

Criteria for Substance Abuse

A. A maladaptive pattern of substance use leading to clinically significant impairment or distress, as manifested by one (or more) of the following, occurring within a 12-month period:

   (1) Recurrent substance use resulting in a failure to fulfill major role obligations at work, school, or home (e.g., repeated absences or poor work performance related to substance use; substance-related absences, suspensions, or expulsions from school; neglect of children or household)

   (2) Recurrent substance use in situations in which it is physically hazardous (e.g., driving an automobile or operating a machine when impaired by substance use)

   (3) Recurrent substance-related legal problems (e.g., arrests for substance-related disorderly conduct)

   (4) Continued substance use despite having persistent or recurrent social or interpersonal problems caused or exacerbated by the

effects of the substance (e.g., arguments with spouse about consequences of intoxication, physical fights)

B. The symptoms have never met the criteria for Substance Dependence
for this class of substance.

Criteria for Substance Dependence

A maladaptive pattern of substance use, leading to clinically significant
impairment or distress, as manifested by three (or more) of the following,
occurring at any time in the same 12-month period:

(1) Tolerance, as defined by either of the following:
   (a) a need for markedly increased amounts of the substance to
   achieve intoxication or desired effect
   (b) markedly diminished effect with continued use of the same
   amount of the substance
(2) Withdrawal, as manifested by either of the following:
   (a) the characteristic withdrawal syndrome for the substance (refer
   to Criteria A and B of the criteria sets for Withdrawal from the
   specific substances)
   (b) the same (or a closely related) substance is taken to relieve or
   avoid withdrawal symptoms
(3) The substance is often taken in larger amounts or over a longer period
   than was intended
(4) There is a persistent desire or unsuccessful efforts to cut down or
   control substance use
(5) A great deal of time is spent in activities necessary to obtain the substance (e.g., visiting multiple doctors or driving long distances), use
   the substance (e.g., chain-smoking), or recover from its effects
(6) Important social, occupational, or recreational activities are given up
   or reduced because of substance use
(7) The substance is continued despite knowledge of having a persistent
   or recurrent physical or psychological problem that is likely to have
   been caused or exacerbated by the substance (e.g., current cocaine
   use despite recognition of cocaine-induced depression, or continued

drinking despite recognition that an ulcer was made worse by alcohol consumption)

Specify if:

    With Physiological Dependence: evidence of tolerance or withdrawal (i.e., neither Item 1 nor 2 is present)

    Without Physiological Dependence: no evidence of tolerance or withdrawal (i.e., neither Item 1 nor 2 is present)

Source: *Diagnostic and Statistical Manual of Mental Disorders: DSM-IV-TR* by American Psychiatric Association Staff. Copyright 2000 in the format Tradebook via Copyright Clearance Center.

Notes

Chapter 1

1 Don Jeffries. *Balm in Gilead* (Little Rock, Ark.: August House Publishers, 1992).

2 J. Rodgers, et al. "Liquid Ecstasy: A New Kid on the Dance Floor," *British Journal of Psychiatry* 184 (2004): 104–106.

3 Andrea Tone, *The Age of Anxiety: A History of America's Turbulent Affair with Tranquilizers* (New York: Basic Books, 2009).

4 Drug Enforcement Administration, "Depressants," http://www.justice.gov/dea/concern/d.html (accessed August 6, 2010).

5 Sean J. Belouin, Pharm.D., Commander, United States Public Health Service, Substance Abuse and Mental Health Services Administration, and Janine Denis Cook, Clinical Chemist, Substance Abuse and Mental Health Services Administration, *Twelve Year Prescribing Trends for Fifteen Different Opioid, Benzodiazepine, Amphetamine, and Barbiturate Prescription Drugs Correlated with Reports of* *Prescription Medication Abuse and Diversion,* Presentation in 2010, http://www.benzos.une.edu/documents/2010/oct11/04_belouin.pdf (accessed on December 17, 2010).

6 Palo Alto Medical Foundation, "Barbiturates," http://www.pamf.org/teen/risk/drugs/depressants/barbiturates.html (accessed February 15, 2011).

7 J. Dave Barry, M.D., and Christopher B. Beach, M.D., "Barbiturate Abuse," http://www.emedicinehealth.com/barbiturate_abuse/page3_em.htm (accessed October 4, 2010).

8 U.S. Army, Fort Jackson, South Carolina, "Army Substance Abuse Program: Civilian Employee Prevention and Training, Part Two," http://www.docstoc.com/docs/38676555/ARMY-SUBSTANCE-ABUSE-PROGRAM9 (accessed October 5, 2010).

9 MedlinePlus, "Barbiturate Intoxication and Overdose," National Institutes of Medicine,

January 14, 2010, http://www
.nlm.nih.gov/medlineplus/
ency/article/000951.htm
(accessed December 22, 2010).

10 MedlinePlus, "Barbiturate
Intoxication and Overdose,"
National Institutes of Medicine,
January 14, 2010, http://www
.nlm.nih.gov/medlineplus/
ency/article/000951.htm
(accessed December 22, 2010).

11 Substance Abuse and Mental
Health Services Administration, *Results from the 2009
National Survey on Drug Use
and Health: Volume I. Summary
of National Findings* (Rockville,
MD: Department of Health and
Human Services, September
2010).

12 Ibid.

13 Adam J. Gordon, *Physical
Illness and Drugs of Abuse: A
Review of the Evidence* (New
York: Cambridge University
Press, 2010).

14 Jay M. Pomerantz, M.D., "Risk
Versus Benefit of Benzodiazepines," *Psychiatric Times* 24, 7
(2007), http://www.psychiatric
times.com/display/article/
10168/55026 (accessed May 25,
2011).

15 Benny Monheit, "Prescription Drug Misuse," *Australian
Family Physician* 39, 8 (2010):
540–546.

16 National Institute of Mental
Health, *Anxiety Disorders,*
http://www.nimh.nih.gov/
health/publications/anxiety-
disorders/nimhanxiety.pdf
(accessed December 12, 2010).

17 Ibid.

18 Jeffrey Susman, M.D., and
Brian Klee, M.D., "The Role of
High-Potency Benzodiazepines
in the Treatment of Panic Disorder," *Primary Care Companion to Journal of Clinical Care
Psychiatry* 7, 1 (2005): 5–11.

19 Monica Williams, "Beating
OCD: When Your Medication
Isn't Doing Enough," University
of Pennsylvania Health System,
http://www.ocdproject.org/
augmenting.php (accessed
December 21, 2010).

20 Jean-Marc Cloos, M.D., "Benzodiazepines and Addiction:
Myths and Realities (Part 1,"
Psychiatric Times July 2010,
https://www.cmellc.com/
CMEActivities/tabid/54/ctl/
ActivityController/mid/545/
activityid/2007/Default.aspx
(accessed December 21, 2010).

21 Matt Jeffereys, M.D., "Clinician's Guide to Medications
for PTSD," National Center for
PTSD, United States Department of Veterans Affairs, http://
www.ptsd.va.gov/professional/
pages/clinicians-guide-to-

medications-for-ptsd.asp
(accessed May 30, 2011).

22 National Drug Intelligence
Center, "GHB and Analogs
Fast Facts," January 1, 2006,
http://www.justice.gov/
ndic/pubs4/4532/index.htm
(accessed May 27, 2011).

23 Drug Enforcement Administration. "Drugs: GHB." Available
online at http://www.getsmart
aboutdrugs.com/drugs/ghb
.html. (accessed June 21, 2011).

24 Esther Gwinnell, M.D., and
Christine Adamec, *The Encyclo-
pedia of Drug Abuse* (New York:
Facts On File, 2008).

25 L.D. Johnston, et al., *Monitoring
the Future: National Results on
Adolescent Drug Use, Overview
of Key Findings,* Institute for
Social Research at the University of Michigan, February
2011.

26 Office on Women's Health,
"Date Rape Drugs," Washing-
ton, D.C.: U.S. Department of
Health and Human Services,
December 5, 2008.

27 Lawrence P. Carter, et al., "Illicit
Gamma-Hydroxybutyrate
(GHB) and Pharmaceuti-
cal Sodium Oxybate (Xrem):
Differences in Characteristics
and Misuse," *Drug and Alcohol
Dependence* 104 (2009): 1–10.

28 Ibid.

29 National Institute of Neurological Disorders and Stroke,
"NINDS Narcolepsy Information Page," May 14, 2010, http://
www.ninds.nih.gov/disorders/
narcolepsy/narcolepsy.htm
(accessed May 25, 2011).

30 Johnston, et al., *Monitoring the
Future: National Results on Adolescent Drug Use,* February 2011.

31 Office on Women's Health,
"Date Rape Drugs," December
5, 2008.

32 MedlinePlus, "Chloral Hydrate,"
February 1, 2009, http://www
.nlm.nih.gov/medlineplus/
druginfo/meds/a682201.html
(accessed May 25, 2011).

33 Drug Enforcement Administration, "Glutethimide & Methaqualone," http://www.justice
.gov/dea.concern/glutethimide
.html (accessed May 23, 2011).

34 A.G. Rowland, et al., "Review of
the Efficacy of Rectal Paraldehyde in the Management of
Acute and Prolonged Tonic-
Clonic Convulsions," *Archives
of the Disabled Child* 94, 9
(2009): 720–723.

35 WHO Expert Committee on
Drug Dependence, Twenty-fifth
Report, World Health Organization. Geneva, 1989, http://
whqlibdoc.who.int/trs/WHO_
TRS_775.pdf (accessed May 24,
2011).

Chapter 2

1 David Young, "Barbiturates," April 10, 2007, faculty.smu.edu/jbuynak/BARBITURATES.ppt (accessed October 5, 2010).

2 Nobelprize.org, "The Nobel Prize in Chemistry, 1905: Adolf von Baeyer," http://nobelprize .org/nobel_prizes/chemistry/laureates/1905 (accessed May 23, 2011); Francisco López-Muñoz, Ronaldo Ucha-Udabe, and Cecilio Alamo, "The History of Barbiturates a Century After Their Clinical Introduction," *Neuropsychiatric Disease and Treatment* 1, 4 (2005): 329–343.

3 Dimitri A. Cozanitis, M.D., "One Hundred Years of Barbiturates and Their Saint," *Journal of the Royal Society of Medicine* 97 (2004): 594–598.

4 Michael Tregenza, "Preparations for Euthanasia in Nazi Germany 1938–1939," *Journal of Pre-Clinical and Clinical Research* 4, 1 (2010), http://www.jpccr.eu/archive_pdf/2010_vol_4_nr_1/jpccr_79 .pdf (accessed May 24, 2011).

5 C.R. Woolf, M.D., "Drugs in the Treatment of Asthma," *Canadian Medical Association Journal* 91 (1964): 77–72.

6 Charles O. Jackson, "Before the Drug Culture; Barbiturate/ Amphetamine Abuse in American Society," *Clio Medica* 11, 1 (1976): 47–58.

7 López-Muñoz, et al., "The History of Barbiturates a Century After Their Clinical Introduction," 335.

8 H.T. Roper-Hall, "The Barbiturates: Their Chemistry, Action, and Toxicology." *Proceedings of the Royal Society of Medicine* 29, 275 (1935): 13–19.

9 Ibid.

10 Oliver F. Bush, M.D., "The Clinical Use of Barbiturates," *Southern Medical Journal* 45, 6 (1952): 553–555.

11 William R. Greene, M.D., and William H. Davis, M.D., "Titrated Intravenous Barbiturates in the Control of Symptoms in Patients with Terminal Cancer," *Southern Medical Journal* 84, 3 (1991): 332–337.

12 Jackson, "Before the Drug Culture," 50.

13 Jackson, "Before the Drug Culture," 47–58.

14 Toine Pieters and Stephen Snelders, "From King Kong Pills to Mother's Little Helpers— Career Cycles of Two Families of Psychotropic Drugs: The Barbiturates and Benzodiazepines," *Canadian Bulletin of Medical History* 24, 1 (2007): 93–112.

15 Jackson, "Before the Drug Culture," 47–58.

16 Burness E. Moore, "The Contribution of Anesthesia to Psychiatry," *Yale Journal of Biology and Medicine* 19, 2 (1946): 195–206.

17 Moore, "The Contribution of Anesthesia to Psychiatry," 203.

18 Maria Naples, and Thomas P. Hackett, M.D., "The Amytal Interview: History and Current Uses," *Psychosomatics* 19, 2 (1978): 98–105.

19 Ronald M. Doctor, Ada P. Kahn, and Christine Adamec, *The Encyclopedia of Phobias, Fears, and Anxieties* (New York: Facts On File, 2008).

20 Naples and Hackett, "The Amytal Interview: History and Current Uses," 98–105.

21 Anil Minocha, M.D., and Christine Adamec, *The Encyclopedia of the Digestive System and Digestive Disorders* (New York: Facts On File, 2011).

22 Laura Calkins, "Detained and Drugged: A Brief Overview of the Use of Pharmaceuticals for the Interrogation of Suspects, Prisoners, Patients, and POWs in the U.S.," *Bioethics* 24, 1 (2010): 27–34.

23 Edward Shorter, *Before Prozac: The Troubled History of Mood Disorders in Psychiatry* (New York: Oxford University Press, 2009).

24 Calkins, "Detained and Drugged," 27–34.

25 American Medical Association Committee on Alcoholism and Addiction, "Dependence on Barbiturates and Other Sedative Drugs," *Journal of the American Medical Association* 193, 8 (1965): 673–677.

26 Frank Wells, "The Moral Choice in Prescribing Barbiturates," *Journal of Medical Ethics* 2 (1976): 68–70.

27 Committee on Public Health, New York Academy of Medicine, "Misuse of Valuable Therapeutic Agents: Barbiturates, Tranquilizers, and Amphetamines," *Bulletin of the New York Academy of Medicine* 40, 12 (1964): 972–979.

28 Harris Isbell, M.D., and H.F. Fraser, M.D., "Addiction to Analgesics and Barbiturates," *Pharmacologic Reviews* 2, 2 (1950): 355–397.

29 Ibid.

30 Jackson, "Before the Drug Culture," 47–58.

31 Andrea Tone, *The Age of Anxiety: A History of America's Turbulent Affair with Tranquilizers* (New York: Basic Books, 2009).

32 Jackson, "Before the Drug Culture," 47–58.

33 Oliver F. Bush, M.D., "The Clinical Use of the Barbitu-

rates," *Southern Medical Journal* 45, 6: (1951): 553–555.

34 Jackson, "Before the Drug Culture," 55.

35 U.S. Congress, Senate Committee on Labor and Public Welfare, Subcommittee on Health, *Barbiturate Abuse in the United States, 1973 Hearing, Ninety-Third Congress, First Session on Examination of Proposed Actions to Combat Barbiturate Abuse in the United States,* May 7, 1973.

36 U.S. Congress, *Barbiturate Abuse in the United States, 1973 Hearing,* 160.

37 Malcolm C. Cumberlidge, "The Abuse of Barbiturates by Heroin Addicts," *Canadian Medical Association Journal* 98 (1968): 1045–1049.

38 R. Gokhale, "Use of Barbiturates in the Treatment of Cyclic Vomiting During Childhood," *Journal of Pediatric Gastroenterology & Nutrition* 25, 1 (1997): 64–67.

39 Ibid.

40 D.F. Scott, and Michael Swash, "Febrile Convulsions in Early Childhood," *British Medical Journal* 3, 5283 (August 12, 1972): 415–416, http://www .bmj.com/content/3/5823.toc (accessed on August 31, 2011).

41 Sean J. Belouin, Pharm.D., Commander, United States Public Health Service, Substance Abuse and Mental Health Services Administration, and Janine Denis Cook, Clinical Chemist, Substance Abuse and Mental Health Services Administration, *Twelve Year Prescribing Trends for Fifteen Different Opioid, Benzodiazepine, Amphetamine, and Barbiturate Prescription Drugs Correlated with Reports of Prescription Medication Abuse and Diversion,* Presentation in 2010, http://www.benzos.une.edu/ documents/2010/oct11/04_ belouin.pdf (accessed on December 17, 2010).

42 Shorter, *Before Prozac.*

43 Susan L. Speaker, "From 'Happiness Pills' to 'National Nightmare': Changing Cultural Assessment of Minor Tranquilizers in America, 1955–1960," *Journal of the History of Medicine* 52 (1997): 338–376.

44 Tone, *The Age of Anxiety.*

45 Ibid.

46 Ibid.

47 Speaker, "From 'Happiness Pills' to 'National Nightmare'," 338–376.

48 Malcolm Lader, "History of Benzodiazepine Dependence," *Journal of Substance Abuse Treatment* 8 (1991): e53–59.

49 Tone, *The Age of Anxiety.*

50 Ibid.

51 Ibid.

52 Matt Herper. "Valium Inventor Leo Sternbach Dies at 97," *Forbes,* October 3, 2005, http://www.forbes.com/2005/10/03/valium-inventor-dies-cx_mh_1003autofacescan03.html (accessed May 26, 2011).

53 Shorter, *Before Prozac.*

54 Pieters and Snelders, "Career Cycles of Two Families of Psychotropic Drugs: The Barbiturates and Benzodiazepines," 104.

55 Shorter, *Before Prozac.*

56 Speaker, "From 'Happiness Pills to 'National Nightmare,'" 338–376.

57 Ibid.

58 Elisa Cascade, and Amir H. Kalali, M.D., "Use of Benzodiazepines in the Treatment of Anxiety," *Psychiatry* 5, 9 (2008): 21–22.

59 Dimitri A. Cozanitis, M.D. "One Hundred Years of Barbiturates and Their Saint." *Journal of the Royal Society of Medicine* 97 (2004): 594–598.

60 Judith C. Barker, Shana L. Harris and Jo E. Dyer. "Experiences of Gamma Hydroxybutyrate (GHB) Ingestion: A Focus Group." *Journal of Psychoactive Drugs* 39, 2 (2007): 115–129.

61 LAR Stein, et al., "A Web-Based Study of Gamma Hydroxybutyrate (GHB): Patterns, Experiences, and Functions of Use," *American Journal of Addiction* 20, 1 (2011): 20–39.

62 Willem M.A. Verhoeven and Siegfried Tuinier. "Serenics: Anti-Aggression Drugs Throughout History." *Clinical Neuropsychiatry* 4 (2007): 135–143.

63 Francisco López-Muñoz, Ronaldo Ucha-Udabe, and Cecilio Alamo, "The History of Barbiturates a Century After Their Clinical Introduction," *Neuropsychiatric Disease and Treatment* 1, 4 (2005): 329–343.

64 Marcia L. Buck, PharmD., "The Use of Chloral Hydrate in Infants and Children," October 3, 2005, http://www.medscape.com/viewarticle/513402 (accessed May 26, 2011).

65 Francisco López-Muñoz, Ronaldo Ucha-Udabe, and Cecilio Alamo, "The History of Barbiturates a Century After Their Clinical Introduction," *Neuropsychiatric Disease and Treatment* 1, 4 (2005): 329–343.

Chapter 3

1 "Gamma-Aminobuytric Acid (GABA)," *Alternative Medicine Review* 12, 3 (2007): 274–279.

2 Guillaume Vaiva, et al., "Low Post-Trauma GABA Plasma Levels as a Predictive Factor

in the Developmenet of Acute Posttraumatic Stress Disorder," *Biological Psychiatry* 55 (2004): 250–254.

3 Roopa Bhatt, et al., "Inhibitory Role for GABA in Autoimmune Inflammation," *PNAS* 107, 6 (2010): 2580–2585.

4 D.G. Murphy, et al., "Autism in Adults. New Biological Findings and Their Translational Implications to the Cost of Clinical Services." *Brain Research* 1380 (2011): 22–33.

5 David A. McCormick, "GABA as an Inhibitory Neurotransmitter in Human Cerebral Cortex," *Journal of Neurophysiology* 62, 3 (1989): 1018–1027.

6 Adam J. Gordon, *Physical Illness and Drugs of Abuse: A Review of the Evidence* (New York: Cambridge University Press, 2010).

7 K. Otani, "Cytochrome P450 3A4 and Benzodiazepines," *Seishin Shinkeigaku Zasshi* 105, 5 (2003): 641–642.

8 Gordon, *Physical Illness and Drugs of Abuse.*

9 Charlotte D'Hulst, John R. Atack, and R. Frank Kooy, "The Complexity of the GABA$_A$ Receptor Shapes Unique Pharmacological Profiles," *Drug Discovery Today* 14, 17–19 (2008): 866–875.

10 Michael H. Nelson, "Sedative-Hypnotic Drugs," http://pharmacy.wingate.edu/faculty/mnelson/PDF/Sedative_Hypnotics.pdf (accessed February 15, 2011).

11 National Institute on Drug Abuse, "CNS Depressants," http://www.nida.nih.gov/researchreports/prescription/prescription3.html (accessed February 10, 2011).

12 "Benzodiazepines: Revisiting Clinical Issues in Treating Anxiety Disorders," *Primary Care Companion to the Journal of Clinical Psychiatry* 7, 1 (2005): 23–30.

13 WebMD, "Barbiturate Abuse," August 10, 2005, http://www.webmd.com/mental-health/barbiturate-abuse (accessed February 15, 2011).

14 Michael H. Nelson, "Sedative-Hypnotic Drugs," http://pharmacy.wingate.edu/faculty/mnelson/PDF/Sedative_Hypnotics.pdf (accessed February 15, 2011).

15 National Committee of Quality Assurance, "Drugs to be Avoided in the Elderly," http://www.ncqa.org/Portals/0/Newsroom/2007/Drugs_Avoided_Elderly.pdf (accessed February 11, 2011).

16 Robert L. Page, et al., "Inappropriate Prescribing in the

Hospitalized Elderly Patient: Defining the Problem, Evaluation Tools, and Possible Solutions," *Clinical Interventions in Aging* 5 (2010): 75–87.

17 Pam G. Harrison, "Barbiturates Still Drugs of Choice in Geriatric Suicide," March 11, 2010, *Medscape Medical News,* http://www.medscape.com/viewarticle/718354_print (accessed October 5, 2010).

18 Mohammed I. Ramadan, M.D., Steve F. Werder, D.O., and Sheldon H.Preskorn, M.D., "Safe Use of Benzodiazepines, Buspirone, and Propranolol," *Journal of Family Practice* 5, 5 (2006), http://www.jfponline.com/Pages.asp?AID=4065 (accessed February 11, 2011).

19 Delmarva Foundation, "Hedis 2009: Drugs to Avoid in the Elderly (DAE)," http://www.mdqio.org/providers/patientSafety/drugSafety/documents/FINAL_Hedis%202009_DAE.pdf (accessed December 29, 2010).

20 Highmark Health Insurance Company, "Drugs to Avoid in the Elderly," https://www.msbcbs.com/PDFFiles/Drugs-to-avoid-in-the-elderly.pdf (accessed December 29, 2010).

21 Robert L. Page, et al., "Inappropriate Prescribing in the Hospitalized Elderly Patient: Defining the Problem, Evaluation Tools, and Possible Solutions," *Clinical Interventions in Aging* 5 (2010): 75–87.

22 National Institutes of Health, "Barbiturate Intoxication and Overdose," June 25, 2010, http://www.nlm.nih.gov/medlineplus/ency/article/000951.htm (accessed September 12, 2010).

23 Ian R. Tebbett, *Drugs of Abuse: A Pharmacist's Guide* (Gainesville, Fla.: University of Florida, 2008).

24 Substance Abuse and Mental Health Services Administration, Office of Applied Studies, "Drug Abuse Warning Network, 2007: National Estimates of Drug-Related Emergency Department Visits," May 2010, https://dawninfo.samhsa.gov/files/ED2007/DAWN2k7ED.pdf (accessed January 10, 2011).

25 Andrew R. Breton, et al., "Follow-up Services After an Emergency Department Visit for Substance Abuse," *American Journal of Managed Care* 13, 9 (2007): 497–505.

26 Substance Abuse and Mental Health Services Administration, Office of Applied Studies, "Drug Abuse Warning Network, 2007: National Estimates of Drug-Related Emergency Department Visits," May 2010,

https://dawninfo.samhsa.gov/files/ED2007/DAWN2k7ED.pdf (accessed January 10, 2011).

27 MedlinePlus, "Barbiturate Intoxication and Overdose," National Institutes of Medicine, January 14, 2010, http://www.nlm.nih.gov/medlineplus/ency/article/000951.htm (accessed December 22, 2010).

28 J. Dave Barry, M.D., and Christopher B. Beach, M.D., "Barbiturate Abuse," http://www.emedicinehealth.com/barbiturate_abuse/page3_em.htm (accessed October 4, 2010).

29 Joan Keegan, et al., "Addiction in Pregnancy," *Journal of Addictive Diseases* 29 (2010): 175–191.

30 Committee on Public Health, New York Academy of Medicine, "Misuse of Valuable Therapeutic Agents: Barbiturates, Tranquilizers, and Amphetamines," *Bulletin of the New York Academy of Medicine* 40, 12 (1964): 974.

31 C. Uhlmann, and W. Froscher, "Low Risk of Development of Substance Dependence for Barbiturates and Clobazam Prescribed as Antiepiletpic Drugs: Results from a Questionnaire Study," *CNS Neuroscience Therapy* 15, 1 (2009): 24–31.

32 Substance Abuse and Mental Health Services Administration, Office of Applied Studies, "Drug Abuse Warning Network, 2007: National Estimates of Drug-Related Emergency Department Visits," May 2010, https://dawninfo.samhsa.gov/files/ED2007/DAWN2k7ED.pdf (accessed January 10, 2011).

33 Centers for Disease Control and Prevention, *Morbidity and Mortality Weekly* 59 (2010): 705–709.

34 Christine Adamec, "Drugs That Contain Barbiturates," Live strong.com Blog, July 21, 2010, http://www.livestrong.com/article/180944-drugs-that-contain-barbiturates (accessed December 27, 2010).

35 Ian R.Tebbett, *Drugs of Abuse: A Pharmacist's Guide* (Gainesville, Fla.: University of Florida, 2008).

36 Liz Thomas, "Barbiturate Withdrawal," Morning Report, March 4, 2008, www.med.unc.edu/medicine/web/3.4.08%20Thomas.ppt (accessed December 22, 2010).

37 Edward M. Sellers, M.D., "Alcohol, Barbiturate and Benzodiazepine Withdrawal Syndromes: Clinical Management," *Canadian Medical Association Journal* 139 (July 15, 1988): 113–118.

38 Substance Abuse and Mental Health Services Administration, Office of Applied Studies, "Drug Abuse Warning Network, 2007: National Estimates of Drug-Related Emergency Department Visits," May 2010, https://dawninfo.samhsa.gov/files/ED2007/DAWN2k7ED.pdf (accessed January 10, 2011).

39 Emily Piercefield, M.D., et al., "Increase in Unintentional Medication in Overdose Deaths: Oklahoma, 1994–2006," *American Journal of Preventive Medicine* 39, 4 (2010): 357–363.

40 Aron J. Hall, et al., "Patterns of Abuse Among Unintentional Pharmaceutical Overdose Fatalities," *Journal of the American Medical Association* 300, 22 (December 10, 2008): 2613–2620.

41 Penny Buykx, et al., "Medications Used in Overdose and How They Are Acquired—An Investigation of Cases Attending an Inner Mebourne Emergency Department," *Australian and New Zealand Journal of Public Health* 34, 4 (2010): 401–404.

42 Substance Abuse and Mental Health Services Administration, Office of Applied Studies, "Drug Abuse Warning Network, 2007: National Estimates of Drug-Related Emergency Department Visits," May 2010, https://dawninfo.samhsa.gov/files/ED2007/DAWN2k7ED.pdf (accessed January 10, 2011).

43 Roland R. Griffiths, and Matthew W. Johnson. "Relative Abuse Liability of Hypnotic Drugs: A Conceptual Framework and Algorithm for Differentiating Among Compounds." *Journal of Clinical Psychiatry* 66, 9 (2005): 31–41.

44 National Institute on Drug Abuse, "Club Drugs (GHB, Ketamine, and Rohypnol)," July 2010, http://www.nida.nih.gov/pdf/infofacts/ClubDrugs10.pdf (accessed May 26, 2011).

45 Judith C. Barker, Shana L. Harris and Jo E. Dyer. "Experiences of Gamma Hydroxybutryrate (GHB) Ingestion: A Focus Group." *Journal of Psychoactive Drugs* 39, 2 (2007): 115–129.

46 National Institute on Drug Abuse, "Club Drugs (GHB, Ketamine, and Rohypnol)," July 2010, http://www.nida.nih.gov/pdf/infofacts/ClubDrugs10.pdf (accessed May 26, 2011).

Chapter 4

1 Li-Tzy Wu, Daniel J. Pilowsky, and Ashwin A. Patkar, "Non-Prescribed Use of Pain Relievers among Adolescents in the United States," *Drug and*

Alcohol Dependence 1, 94 (2008): 1–11.

2   National Institutes of Health, "Barbiturate Intoxication and Overdose," June 25, 2010, http://www.nlm.nih.gov/ medlineplus/ency/article/ 000951.htm (accessed June 8, 2011).

3   Charles P. O'Brien, M.D., "Benzodiazepine Use, Abuse, and Dependence," *Journal of Clinical Psychiatry* 66, suppl. 2 (2005): 28–33.

4   Charles E. Romero, M.D., et al., "Barbiturate Withdrawal Following Internet Purchase of Fioricet," *Archives of Neurology* 61 (2004): 1111–1112.

5   Anna A. Theodorou, et al. "Recent Trends in Utilization of Antianxiety Medication." *American Journal of Pharmacy Benefits* 1, 4 (2009): 225–339.

6   Raj K. Kalapatapu, M.D., and Maria A. Sullivan, M.D., "Prescription Use Disorders in Older Adults," *American Journal on Addictions* 19 (2010): 515–522.

7   "Detection of Benzodiazepine Dependence in the Elderly," *RGH Pharmacy E-Bulletin* 38, 12 (July 19, 2010), http://www .auspharmacist.net.au/ ebulletin/vol38/eb38–12.pdf (accessed January 16, 2011).

8   Greg Neale, and Allan J. Smith, "Self-Harm and Suicide Asso-

ciated with Benzodiazepine Usage," *British Journal of General Practice* (2007): 407–408.

9   Heather Ashton, "The Diagnosis and Management of Benzodiazepine Dependence," *Current Opinion in Psychiatry* 18 (2005): 249–255.

10 Ibid.

11 Ibid.

12 Jean-Marc Cloos, M.D., "Benzodiazepines and Addiction: Myths and Realities (Part 1," *Psychiatric Times* July 2010, https://www.cmellc.com/ landing/pdf/A10001071.pdf (accessed December 21, 2010).

13 Jay M. Pomerantz, M.D., "Risk Versus Benefit of Benzodiazepines." *Psychiatric Times* 24, 7 (2007), http://www.psychiatric times.com/display/article/ 10168/55026 (accessed May 25, 2011).

14 Ibid.

15 Susan Y. Kim, harm. D., et al. "High-Risk Behaviors and Hospitalizations Among Gamma Hydroxybutyrate (GHB) Users," *American Journal of Drug and Alcohol Abuse* 33, 3 (2007): 429–438.

16 World Health Organization, *WHO Expert Committee on Drug Dependence. Twenty-fifth Report,* Geneva, 1989.

17 Drug Enforcement Administration, "Drug Information: P,"

http://www.justice.gov/dea/
concern/p.html (accessed
April 29, 2011).

Chapter 5

1 National Institute of Drug
   Abuse, *Principles of Drug Addic-*
   tion Treatment: A Research-
   Based Guide, Second Edition
   (Washington, D.C.: National
   Institutes of Health, May 2009).
2 M. Lader, A. Tylee, and J. Don-
   oghue, "Withdrawing Benzodiazepines in Primary Care," *CNS*
   Drugs 23, 1 (2009): 19034.
3 John Marks, "The Benzodiazepines—For Good or Evil,"
   Neuropsychobiology 10 (1983):
   115–126.
4 Edward M. Sellers, M.D.,
   "Alcohol, Barbiturate and Benzodiazepine Withdrawal Syndromes: Clinical Management,"
   Canadian Medical Association
   Journal 139 (July 15, 1988):
   113–118.
5 Eric Khong, Moira G. Sim,
   and Gary Hulse, "Benzodiazepine Dependence," *Australian*
   Family Physician 33, 11 (2004):
   923–926.
6 Richard C. Oude Voshaar,
   M.D., et al. "Predictors of
   Long-Term Benzodiazepine
   Abstinence in Participants
   of a Randomized Controlled
   Benzodiazepine Withdrawal
   Program," *Canadian Journal*

of Psychiatry 51, 7 (2006):
445–452.
7 Gerard J. Connors, Dennis M.
   Donovan, and Carlo C. DeCle-
   mente, *Substance Abuse Treat-*
   ment and the Stages of Change:
   Selecting and Planning Inter-
   ventions (New York: Guilford
   Press, 2004).
8 National Institute of Mental
   Health, "Psychotherapies,"
   http://www.nimh.nih.gov/
   health/topics/psychotherapies/
   index.shtml (accessed February 12, 2011).
9 Substance Abuse and Mental
   Health Services Administration, "Clinical or Therapeutic
   Approaches Used by Substance
   Abuse Treatment Facilities,"
   N-SSATS Report (October 14,
   2010), http://www.oas.samhsa
   .gov/2k10/238/238ClinicalAp
   2k10Web.pdf (accessed January 10, 2011).
10 Ibid.
11 National Institute of Mental
    Health, "Psychotherapies,"
    http://www.nimh.nih.gov/
    health/topics/psychotherapies/
    index.shtml (accessed Febru-
    ary 12, 2011).
12 Substance Abuse and Mental
    Health Services Administra-
    tion, "Clinical or Therapeutic
    Approaches Used by Substance
    Abuse Treatment Facilities,"
    N-SSATS Report (October 14,

2010), http://www.oas.samhsa
.gov/2k10/238/238ClinicalAp
2k10Web.pdf (accessed January 10, 2011).

13 Ibid.

14 Anne Zahradnik, et al., "Randomized Controlled Trial of a Brief Intervention for Problematic Prescription Drug Use in Non-Treatment-Seeking Patients," *Addiction* 104 (2009): 109–117.

15 Eric Khong, Moira G. Sim, and Gary Hulse, "Benzodiazepine Dependence," *Australian Family Physician* 33, 11 (2004): 923–926.

16 National Institute of Drug Abuse, *Principles of Drug Addiction Treatment: A Research-Based Guide,* Second Edition (Washington, D.C.: National Institutes of Health, May 2009).

Chapter 6

1 National Forensic Laboratory Information System, Drug Enforcement Administration, *NFLIS Special Report: Controlled Substance Prescription Drugs, 2001–2005,* November 2006. http://www.deadiversion .usdoj.gov/nflis/2006rx_drugs_ report.pdf (accessed December 29, 2010).

2 Office of Diversion Control, Drug Enforcement Administration, "Drugs and Chemicals of Concern: Benzodiazepines," December 2010, http://www .deadiversion.usdoj.gov/ drugs_concern/benzo_1.htm (accessed December 17, 2010).

3 Federal Bureau of Prisons, *Detoxification of Chemically Dependent Inmates,* August 2009, http://www.bop.gov/ news/PDFs/detoxification.pdf (accessed December 20, 2010).

4 C. Postigo, M.L. de Alda, and D. Barceló, "Evaluation of Drugs of Abuse Use and Trends in a Prison Through Wastewater Analysis," *Environment International* 367, 1 (2011): 49–55.

5 Lawrence P. Carter, et al. "Illicit Gamma-Hydroxybutyrate (GHB) and Pharmaceutical Sodium Oxybate (Xrem): Differences in Characteristics and Misuse." *Drug and Alcohol Dependence* 104 (2009): 1–10.

6 Drug Enforcement Administration, "Rohypnol (Flunitrazepam)," http://www.justice.gov/ dea/concern/flunitrazepam .html (accessed May 27, 2011).

7 Office on Women's Health, "Date Rape Drugs," Washington, D.C.: U.S. Department of Health and Human Services, December 5, 2008.

8 Office on Women's Health, "Date Rape Drugs," Washing-

ton, D.C.: U.S. Department of Health and Human Services, December 5, 2008.

Chapter 7

1 Drug Enforcement Administration, "Barbiturates," http://www.justice.gov/dea/concern/b.html (accessed August 6, 2010).

2 Mohammad Tahir Hussain, and Steven A. Shea, "Wake Up to Insomnia: Future Approaches to the Management of Insomnia," *Nature and Science of Sleep* 3 (2011): 33–35.

3 S. Hood, "The Role of Flumazenil in the Treatment of Benzodiazepine Dependence: Physiological and Psychological Profiles," *Journal of Psychopharmacology* 23, 4 (2009): 401–409.

4 S. Hood, G. O'Neil, and G. Hulse, "The Role of Flumazenil in the Treatment of Benzodiazepine Dependence: Physiological and Psychological Profiles," *Journal of Psychopharmacology* 23 (2009): 401–409.

5 P. Oulis, and G. Konstantakopoulos, "Pregabalin in the Treatment of Alcohol and Benzodiazepine Dependence," *CNS Neuroscience & Therapeutics* 16 (2010): 45–50.

6 Michael Liebrenz, et al., "Agonist Substitution—A Treatment Alternative for High-Dose Benzodiazepine-Dependent Patients?" *Addiction* 105 (2010): 1870–1874.

7 Ibid.

8 Ibid.

Glossary

anxiety disorder   A disorder that causes anxiety and other symptoms for more than six months. The primary anxiety disorders are generalized anxiety disorder, obsessive-compulsive disorder, panic disorder, post-traumatic stress disorder, social phobia, and specific phobia. Both barbiturates and benzodiazepines have been used to treat many anxiety disorders, although barbiturates are no longer used for this purpose.

barbiturate   A central nervous system depressant that is prescribed for individuals with sleep difficulties and sometimes for disorders such as epilepsy, and which can be addicting.

barbiturate intoxication   A condition in which the individual experiences such symptoms as staggering, trouble thinking, shallow breathing, and slowed speech.

benzodiazepine   A central nervous system depressant that is prescribed to treat anxiety and which has an addictive potential.

depressant   Medications that cause an inhibition of the central nervous system, often leading to sedation. They are prescribed for those with anxiety or insomnia, such as barbiturates and benzodiazepines. Depressants can also be illicit drugs such as gamma hydroxybutyric acid (GHB).

detoxification   Ending the use of an abusive or addictive substance under the supervision of a physician or in a treatment facility.

doctor shopping   Refers to a patient contacting two or more physicians in order to obtain a prescription for a specific drug they wish to abuse, such as a barbiturate. The patient also fills the prescriptions at different pharmacies to avoid detection of these illegal acts. In most cases, the physicians are unaware of what the patient is doing.

drug diversion   The transfer of a legitimately prescribed drug to another individual, such as when a person is prescribed a barbiturate or benzodiazepine and gives the drug to others. Sometimes the drug is not freely given but is stolen from a medicine cabinet.

105

gamma-aminobutyric acid (GABA)   A neurotransmitter that inhibits the central nervous system, for example, calming a person who is anxious. Both barbiturates and benzodiazepines boost the brain levels of GABA. The term GABA is also used to refer to a depressant drug that is sometimes abused in the United States.

taper   To reduce the use of an addicting drug under the supervision of a physician, rather than abruptly discontinuing its use. An abrupt withdrawal from a barbiturate or benzodiazepine may cause severe side effects.

therapeutic-to-toxic range   The difference between an efficacious use of a drug and a dangerous use. In the case of barbiturates there is a narrow therapeutic-to-toxic range, which means that if a person even slightly increases the dosage, then the drug may cause coma and even death. This is not true for benzodiazepines.

tolerance   The need to take greater amounts of a drug to achieve the same effects as in the past. Tolerance can be an indicator of abuse or addiction; however, other indicators must also be present, such as an intense craving for the drug.

further Resources

Books and Articles

Ashton, Heather. "The Diagnosis and Management of Benzodiazepine Dependence." *Current Opinion in Psychiatry* 18 (2005): 249–255.

Cloos, Jean-Marc, M.D. "Benzodiazepines and Addiction: Myths and Realities (Part 1)," *Psychiatric Times*, July 2010. Available online. URL: https://www.cmellc.com/CMEActivities/tabid/54/ctl/ActivityController/mid/545/activityid/2007/Default.aspx. Accessed on December 21, 2010.

Doctor, Ronald M., Ada P. Kahn, and Christine Adamec. *The Encyclopedia of Phobias, Fears, and Anxieties.* New York: Facts On File, 2008.

Gordon, Adam J. *Physical Illness and Drugs of Abuse: A Review of the Evidence.* New York: Cambridge University Press, 2010.

Jackson, Charles O. "Before the Drug Culture: Barbiturate/Amphetamine Abuse in American Society." *Clio Medica* 11, 1 (1976): 47–58.

Kalapatapu, Raj K., M.D., and Maria A. Sullivan, M.D. "Prescription Use Disorders in Older Adults." *American Journal on Addictions* 19 (2010): 515–522.

Keegan, Joan et al. "Addiction in Pregnancy." *Journal of Addictive Diseases* 29 (2010): 175–191.

Lader, Malcolm. "Effectiveness of Benzodiazepines: Do They Work or Not?" *Expert Reviews Neurotherapy* 8, 8 (2008): 1189–1191.

López-Muñoz, Francisco, Ronaldo Ucha-Udabe, and Cecilio Alamo. "The History of Barbiturates a Century After Their Clinical Introduction." *Neuropsychiatric Disease and Treatment* 1, 4 (2005): 329–343.

McCormick, David A. "GABA as an Inhibitory Neurotransmitter in Human Cerebral Cortex." *Journal of Neurophysiology* 62, 3 (1989): 1018–1027.

MedlinePlus. "Barbiturate Intoxication and Overdose," National Institutes of Medicine, January 14, 2010. Available online. URL: http://www.nlm.nih.gov/medlineplus/ency/article/000951.htm. Accessed on December 22, 2010.

Minocha, Anil, M.D., and Christine Adamec. *The Encyclopedia of the Digestive System and Digestive Disorders*. New York: Facts On File, 2011.

Naples, Maria, and Thomas P. Hackett, M.D. "The Amytal Interview: History and Current Uses," *Psychosomatics* 19, 2 (1978): 98–105.

O'Brien, Charles P., M.D. "Benzodiazepine Use, Abuse, and Dependence," *Journal of Clinical Psychiatry* 66, Supp. 2 (2005): 28–33.

Oulis, P., and G. Konstantakopoulos. "Pregabalin in the Treatment of Alcohol and Benzodiazepine Dependence," *CNS Neuroscience & Therapeutics* 16 (2010): 45–50.

Page III, Robert L., et al. "Inappropriate Prescribing in the Hospitalized Elderly Patient: Defining the Problem, Evaluation Tools, and Possible Solutions," *Clinical Interventions in Aging* 5 (2010): 75–87.

Pieters, Toine, and Stephen Snelders. "From King Kong Pills to Mother's Little Helpers—Career Cycles of Two Families of Psychotropic Drugs: The Barbiturates and Benzodiazepines," *Canadian Bulletin of Medical History* 24, 1 (2007): 93–112.

Romero, Charles E., M.D., et al. "Barbiturate Withdrawal Following Internet Purchase of Fioricet," *Archives of Neurology* 61 (2004): 1111–1112.

Roper-Hall, H.T. "The Barbiturates: Their Chemistry, Action, and Toxicology," *Proceedings of the Royal Society of Medicine* 29, 275 (1935): 13–19.

Sellers, Edward M., M.D. "Alcohol, Barbiturate and Benzodiazepine Withdrawal Syndromes: Clinical Management," *Canadian Medical Association Journal* 139 (July 15, 1988): 113–118.

Shorter, Edward. *Before Prozac: The Troubled History of Mood Disorders in Psychiatry*. New York: Oxford University Press, 2009.

Speaker, Susan L. "From 'Happiness Pills' to 'National Nightmare': Changing Cultural Assessment of Minor Tranquilizers in America, 1955–1960," *Journal of the History of Medicine* 52 (1997): 338–376.

Substance Abuse and Mental Health Services Administration. "Clinical or Therapeutic Approaches Used by Substance Abuse Treatment Facilities." *N-SSATS Report* (October 14, 2010). Available online. URL: http://www.oas.samhsa.gov/2k10/238/238ClinicalAp2k10Web.pdf. Accessed on January 10, 2011.

Substance Abuse and Mental Health Services Administration. *Results from the 2009 National Survey on Drug Use and Health: Volume I. Summary of National Findings*. September 2010. Rockville, Md.: Department of Health and Human Services.

Tone, Andrea. *The Age of Anxiety: A History of America's Turbulent Affair with Tranquilizers*. New York: Basic Books, 2009.

Voshaar, Richard C. Oude, M.D., et al. "Predictors of Long-Term Benzodiazepine Abstinence in Participants of a Randomized Controlled Benzodiazepine Withdrawal Program." *Canadian Journal of Psychiatry* 51, 7 (2006): 445–452.

Web Sites

Drug Enforcement Administration
http://www.justice.gov/dea/index.htm
This site discusses drugs of abuse and dependence of concern to the Drug Enforcement Administration, such as drugs listed under the Controlled Substances Act. Barbiturates and benzodiazepines are controlled drugs.

FDA Approved Drugs
http://www.accessdata.fda.gov/scripts/cder/drugsatfda/
This site allows users to type in a brand or generic drug name and receive information about the drug.

Narcotics Anonymous
http://www.na.org
A site that provides support for individuals addicted to all types of drugs and that helps individuals identify meeting areas in local cities.

National Institute of Drug Abuse
http://www.nida.nih.gov/NIDAHome.html
A site that provides information on drugs of abuse.

Substance Abuse and Mental Health Services Administration
http://www.samhsa.gov/
A source that provides information on the abuse of substances such as benzodiazepines, barbiturates, alcohol, and other substances as well as information on mental health issues among substance abusers.

Index

About the Author

Christine Adamec has coauthored many books for Facts On File, Inc., including *The Encyclopedia of Alcoholism and Alcohol Abuse* (2010), *The Encyclopedia of Drug Abuse* (2008), *The Encyclopedia of Phobias, Fears, and Anxieties* (2008), *The Encyclopedia of Child Abuse,* Third Edition (2007), and numerous other titles. In addition, Adamec authored *Pathological Gambling* (2010) for Chelsea House's Psychological Disorders series.

About the Consulting Editor

Consulting editor **David J. Triggle, Ph.D.,** is a SUNY Distinguished Professor and the University Professor at the State University of New York at Buffalo. These are the two highest academic ranks of the university. Professor Triggle received his education in the United Kingdom with a Ph.D. degree in chemistry from the University of Hull. Following postdoctoral fellowships at the University of Ottawa (Canada) and the University of London (United Kingdom) he assumed a position in the School of Pharmacy at the University at Buffalo. He served as chairman of the Department of Biochemical Pharmacology from 1971 to 1985 and as Dean of the School of Pharmacy from 1985 to 1995. From 1996 to 2001 he served as Dean of the Graduate School and from 1999 to 2001 was also the University Provost. He is currently the University Professor, in which capacity he teaches bioethics and science policy, and is President of the Center for Inquiry Institute, a think tank located in Amherst, New York, and devoted to issues around the public understanding of science. In the latter respect he is a major contributor to the online M.Ed. program—"Science and The Public"—in the Graduate School of Education and The Center for Inquiry.